# Take Charge
# of Your Destiny

*Alan N Keiran*
(Matthew 6:33)

## ALAN N. KEIRAN

DESTINY IMAGE® PUBLISHERS, INC.
P.O. Box 310, Shippensburg, PA 17257-0310

*"Speaking to the Purposes of God for this Generation
and for the Generations to Come."*

This book and all other Destiny Image, Revival Press, Mercy Place, Fresh Bread, Destiny Image Fiction, and Treasure House books are available at Christian bookstores and distributors worldwide.

For a U.S. bookstore nearest you, call 1-800-722-6774.
For more information on foreign distributors, call 717-532-3040.
Reach us on the Internet at www.destinyimage.com.

ISBN 10: 0-7684-2735-5
ISBN 13: 978-0-7684-2735-6

For Worldwide Distribution, Printed in the U.S.A.

1 2 3 4 5 6 7 8 9 10 11 / 12 11 10 09 08

# Dedication

I dedicate this book to my wife, Sally, whose encouragement, love, and prayers over the past 34 years have buoyed my spirit during grueling years of graduate study, arduous deployments at sea, and in serving with U.S. Marines in combat in Southwest Asia. Sally's courage "under fire" inspires me to persevere no matter what the enemy of our souls sends against me.

This book is also dedicated to my mother, Claire Keiran, whose love, wisdom, and encouragement taught me by example that true Christian faith is lived humbly in the center of God's ideal will.

Finally, I dedicate this book to our children, Jennifer and John, whose lives are testimonies of God's faithfulness in fulfilling His promise of blessing the children of those who love Him.

Special thanks to Fr. Dan Coughlin, Bishop Joe Estabrook, Bill Johnson, Randy Clark, Jim Tolle, Young Hoon Lee, Dick Peace, Bill Thomas, Bill Jeschke, Jeff Williams, and of course, Bishop Bill Hamon for their kind words.

Special thanks also to those who contributed to this work: Chris Agrisani and Dr. Al Hill for layout and design insights and encouragement; as well as Mark O'Keefe, Chaplain Buck Underwood, Max Kidalov, Moses Jang, and my wife, Sally, for editorial suggestions. This was a team effort from beginning to end.

Special thanks also to our senior pastor at International Calvary Church (ICC) in Springfield, Virginia, Dr. (Sharon)

Sung Ja Lee. Her prayer life, preaching, and evangelistic heart, as well as her dedication to Jesus and His church, are great inspirations to us all.

My final expression of gratitude is to Pastor Hank Kunneman of Lord of Hosts Church in Omaha, Nebraska, who prophesied this book into existence a year before a single word appeared on paper.

As you read this book, may the Lord bless you with deepening fellowship and profound spiritual illumination.

# *Endorsements*

In *Take Charge of Your Destiny*, Alan Keiran paints a wonderful picture of the normal Christian life of victory. In doing so, he offers tools that are sure to help the reader to identify areas of powerlessness, as well as bring confidence and awareness that enable us to take charge of our destiny. Alan has an unusual ability to take the practical aspects of the Christian life and present them in such a way that you can see the divine plan for the everyday world changer.

Bill Johnson
Senior Pastor, Bethel Church, Redding, California
Author, *When Heaven Invades Earth*
and *Face to Face with God*

"Seek first the Kingdom of God" (see Matt. 6:33), is one of the clearest directives Jesus has given to his disciples. *Take Charge of Your Destiny* is not only the personal story of how Alan Keiran answered that call to put God's Kingdom first in his life, but a practical down-to-Earth guide for those who want to follow his example. In a very clear and practical way, Alan explains how to listen to God, the importance of accepting the Lord Jesus as our Savior, our call to glorify God, and our deep need for the guidance and empowerment of the Holy Spirit.

His message is compelling because we face a formidable foe—the enemy of our souls. With God's guidance and anointing, we gain the greatest possible advantage in resisting the devil and honoring God through faithful Kingdom service.

*Take Charge of Your Destiny* strongly reminds us that God has given every follower of Jesus dynamic spiritual authority. When we take ownership of that authority and rightly apply it, God's power works in and through us to overcome every obstacle in establishing God's Kingdom. This is a book for everyone who truly seeks to live as a victorious disciple of Christ, but feels the world's distracting pull. It's a book of hope and empowerment—one that is definitely worth reading.

The Most Reverend Joseph W. Estabrook
Auxiliary Bishop, Catholic Archdiocese
for the Military Services, USA

*Take Charge of Your Destiny* is a powerful book about how to live our lives out of relationship with God—a relationship so close that God speaks to us and directs us. Alan, a career Navy chaplain and now Chief of Staff in the office of the Chaplain of the U.S. Senate, explains how to live a life that can know God's leadings, recognize His promptings, and how to live the more abundant life that comes from fulfilling His destiny for your life. I believe this book is one of the most practical books I have read of late for developing a fulfilling lifestyle. I found the fourteen principles and the action steps at the end of the chapters very helpful for applying the principles. I believe *Take Charge of Your Destiny* will help many people develop a stronger, more victorious life for the glory of God. I liked how the book dealt with fruit and gifts, word and works, discipline and grace, or better yet, how to live in a grace-based, Spirit-led, compassion-empowered discipline. The other type of discipline, legalism, degenerates into powerless religion. The discipline for life in this book is grace based and relational, thrilling, with the possibility to partner with God in life. I highly recommend the book.

Pastor Randy Clark
Founder and President of the
Apostolic Network of Global Awakening
Harrisburg, Pennsylvania

Many authors are telling us how to fulfill our deepest desires. Most fail to teach their readers that God is looking for spiritual warriors—mature men and women of faith whose consecrated hearts are primarily focused on things above rather than earthly gratification, and on glorifying the One who died to save us from our sins rather than our every carnal desire. God doesn't exist just to meet our needs. In fact, we exist to glorify God by fulfilling His plans for our lives as we mature in faith and commitment to loving and serving God.

Pastor Alan Keiran's precious book, *Take Charge of Your Destiny*, clearly articulates the biblical way to please God. The reason this book is so precious is that it includes inspired guiding principles received in spiritual dreams (the gift of prophecy) from the Lord. These guiding principles are holy insights which will help any child of God experience and spread the seeds of spiritual awakening.

I pray that everyone who reads this book will be filled with the Holy Spirit and by extension, becomes equipped to discern between God and the world and to serve God with all their hearts, receiving the wisdom to serve neighbors. Lastly, I earnestly hope that every reader of *Take Charge of Your Destiny* will be inspired to live a life that glorifies Almighty God.

Reverend Young Hoon Lee
Senior Pastor of the one million-member Yoido
Full Gospel Church in Seoul, Korea

Alan Keiran is truly a pastor of souls. He has engaged many people in meaningful conversation while here on Capitol Hill. Now in this book, he leads them to uncover the Kingdom of God within. Step by step he guides the reader to uncover the destiny the Lord has already placed in his or her heart. No matter how busy one may be or how important the work at hand, a person does not need to lose his or her way. With the Lord as a partner every day in every way, one's true destiny will simply unfold. This belief of Alan Keiran is contagious.

Alan Keiran has done us a favor! In *Take Charge of Your Destiny*, he insightfully leads the reader into a wonderful discovery of God as well as into a true discovery of oneself. These two discoveries are not separate, he offers. Instead, they are inextricably linked. As he so rightfully states, a person can never advance toward his or her real purpose in life without knowing the Source of their existence. This is highly recommended reading because of its true practicality for one's life.

Filled with the practical and spiritual wisdom of a pastor and chaplain who has walked with God, Alan Keiran's well-organized book is the life message of a good and godly man. Read it and grow.

I highly recommend Alan Keiran's, *Taking Charge of Your Destiny*. He speaks with authority—because he has lived, endured, and experienced much—about partnering and aligning with God's will; about seeking the Lord for direction and heeding His voice; about seeking *first* the Kingdom of God and His righteousness; about the remarkable liberty and freedom we experience when we surrender our lives to His Kingdom purposes; and about the amazing grace that empowers us to influence others as we partner with Him. I know Alan personally and can attest to the fruit in his life borne of his heart to love and serve people: those in high governmental places, those who are down and out, those who might never visit a church lest they be invited by someone who really loves and cares about people. *Taking Charge of Your Destiny* shows us how to take the vastness of the Kingdom dominion message and apply these truths on a personal basis.

William M. Thomas, CEO, CIBN
Workplace Ministries
Dallas, Texas

Alan Keiran has written a basic book about basic Christian living. What he writes is not esoteric or unattainable. As he says, this is a book about "the normal Christian life." Filled with stories, mostly from his own life, *Take Charge of Your Destiny* reads easily and quickly—though living out the life Dr. Keiran commends will not necessarily come easily and quickly.

Not surprisingly, the book begins by urging the reader to learn to listen to God. The world of sense, sight, and sound is so overwhelming that we need to work at hearing God. And indeed, Dr. Keiran is a great listener. He is a modern mystic who lets us listen in on his ongoing conversation with God by sharing generously from his own journals.

I warmly commend this book as the mature musings of a mature man of God on the kind of life God calls us to lead as his beloved children.

Dr. Richard Peace
Robert Boyd Munger Professor of Evangelism
and Spiritual Formation Fuller Theological Seminary

*Take Charge of Your Destiny* is a reflection of the heart of one of the most inspiring, daring, humble, and obedient Christians I know. I'm not surprised that God chose Alan to write it; not just because he is an effective mouthpiece for God, but because he practices what he preaches. If you had opportunity to spend a day with him, you would get the message of the book by seeing how Alan lives.

Short of that, this book is an accurate glimpse through Alan's heart to the heart of God. Great things happen for God's Kingdom when we dare to take God at His Word by diligently seeking Him and putting into practice what He reveals to us. This book focuses the work of God's Kingdom servants through faithful practice of time-tested spiritual disciplines.

I'm thrilled that this practical, action-oriented guide to living an extraordinary life has been produced because it answers the question many are asking, "Now that I've accepted that life isn't about me, how do I make the most of my life for God?" Alan dared to obey God by writing *Take Charge of Your Destiny*. I pray that you will dare to read it and then put its principles into practice.

Jeff Williams

Professional Leadership, Life, and Marriage Coach;

Master Coach, Trainer, and Clinical Counselor

President of Grace and Truth Relationship

Education and Great Relationships

# Contents

# Foreword
## by Bishop Bill Hamon

According to Dr. Alan Keiran, God's blessings flow into lives when those lives are aligned with His sovereign purposes.

Alan Keiran has written a book God wanted written, because God has sown inspired seed thoughts within the author. When inspired seeds like these are watered by prayer and obedience, they mature until harvest time, when they are penned, printed, and published for a waiting audience.

This book has such an anointed beginning. Alan Keiran heard the voice of God through a series of prophecies (God communicating His thoughts and desires by words) and fourteen spiritual dreams (God communicating by pictures and illustrations). The book's inspiration is confirmed in the clear and firm agreement Alan's ideas, principles, and content share with the Bible, the written word of God. You may read this book of deep truth with confidence. When you do, you will "take charge of your destiny" and bring much glory to God.

The secret to every successful endeavor found in the Bible is men and women hearing—and properly responding to—the voice of God. Thank you, Alan, for hearing and responding yourself, and for giving us these life-changing truths and principles. God will be glorified, and His people edified, by this book.

# Introduction

*God has ordained your destiny.*

That's right! You were created on purpose, for a unique purpose. You have a pre-planned destiny crafted specifically for you by God Almighty. He says, "I know the plans I have for you...plans to prosper you and not to harm you, plans to give you hope and a future" (Jer. 29:11). You are God's workmanship, created in Christ Jesus to do good works, which God prepared in advance for you to do (see Eph. 2:10). God has a plan for your life, but how do you find out what it is and live in it? It's simpler than you may think. Just...

*Take Charge of Your Destiny.*

How do you take charge of your destiny? That's the question this book answers. Each chapter focuses on an essential principle in optimizing your time on Earth by living in the center of God's best plans for your life. You'll learn practical, life-transforming truths that will maximize your positive impact on society as you bring God's Kingdom to Earth one act of joyful obedience at a time.

Why is *your* contribution essential?

God wants your help! He has things for you to do that no one else can do. Since His Kingdom comes where His will is done (see Matt. 6:10), He's asking you to seek first His Kingdom every day and in return, He promises to meet all your needs along the way (see Matt. 6:33). When you seek His Kingdom above all else, you will make the world better, one heart at a time.

Why is your contribution so critical? Jesus is coming back. But before He returns, the Gospel of the Kingdom must reach every nation on this planet. Jesus says, "And this gospel of the kingdom will be preached in the whole world as a testimony to all nations, and then the end will come" (Matt. 24:14).

When the Kingdom message reaches every nation, tribe, and tongue, Jesus will return. Paul tells us, "Then the end will come, when He hands over the kingdom to God the Father after he has destroyed all dominion, authority and power" (1 Cor. 15:24).

The more of us who partner with God in spreading the Good News of the Kingdom at home and abroad, the sooner Jesus will return. Do you want to make a positive impact on humanity? Do you want to be a world changer? Then *Take Charge of Your Destiny* and bring God's Kingdom to Earth one act of obedience at a time.

Follow the *Take Charge of Your Destiny Action Steps* found at the end of each chapter, and with the Holy Spirit's help, you'll see God's Kingdom come to Earth through your acts of joyous service and sincere devotion.

# CHAPTER 1

# Listen to God

*Show me Your ways, O Lord, teach me Your paths; guide me in Your truth and teach me, for You are God my Savior, and my hope is in You all day long. —King David* (Psalm 25:4-5)

The Lord is teaching you...It all comes by recognizing His voice and listening to it, "hearkening" the Bible would say. How can God talk with souls that do not recognize His voice when He does speak? In the nature of things it is impossible.[1] —Hannah Whitall Smith

God loves you absolutely, unabashedly, unconditionally.

He wants nothing but the very best for you and those you love. Fulfilling your destiny is His highest goal for your life. But you'll need His help to reach that zenith. He's ready to reveal His life-enhancing plans to you, but...

*Are you listening?*

Listening attentively to God will bring you into your destiny, spare you from mountains of heartache, and save you from an uncertain future. It will also bring you into the deepest intimacy with God that's possible on this side of eternity. Nothing will satisfy you more than experiencing the Father heart of God. You are called to seek His presence and obey His guidance. You'll discover His amazing plans for your life by taking time to listen for Him to speak. That's how you stay in the center of God's will and on track to your destiny.

Listening to God during the first Gulf War certainly kept me on track to my destiny.

My Marine Corps unit deployed to Saudi Arabia in early December '91. By the time allied forces invaded Kuwait, the Marines and sailors of the Sixth Marine Regiment had endured all the waiting we could stand.

At dawn, our convoy finally crossed the Kuwaiti border, successfully navigating two minefields and narrowly avoiding enemy artillery and mortar rounds exploding nearby.

All day we inched along, so hyped from anticipating attack that we could barely sip the heavily chlorinated water in our canteens. Minutes seemed like hours in the choking dust, merciless heat, and oil-laden smoke. The relentless stress was exhausting.

That evening the Iraqis opened fire. As tracers flew toward us, the inky darkness obliterated any hope of rapid escape. We dove for cover behind our darkened vehicles.

Chaplains never carry weapons in combat, so I depended on my assistant for protection. As he crouched nearby, I sat in wet sand with my back to our front tire. Marines with night-vision goggles engaged the enemy in a brief, but decisive, firefight. I was about to climb back into our truck when I heard God say in a clearly articulated thought, *"Aim your flashlight ahead of your vehicle."*

When I did, the narrow red beam revealed the detonator of a mine sticking out of the sand just two feet in front of our truck. We were in a minefield and didn't know it. It's miraculous that no one accidentally triggered a deadly explosion.

After carefully navigating around the mines, we left the area without further incident. God clearly communicated with me that night and saved us from possible injury or death.

God is still speaking, but why doesn't everyone hear His voice? That's because many people aren't taking time to listen to God!

Are you listening? You should be, because unless you listen attentively to God, your life will have no ultimate meaning. Why? Because God sees your life from a very different perspective than you do. Yours is a temporal perspective; His is an eternal one.

What more can you hope to experience if you listen attentively to God and do what He directs? Deep joy, peace, love, and fulfillment; a sense of His abiding presence; and specific guidance to help you take charge of your destiny.

## WHAT DOES IT MEAN TO TAKE CHARGE OF YOUR DESTINY?

Taking charge of your destiny means following God's plans for your life, not just your own. It's living God's way every day for His glory.

Your best possible life on Earth is found in the center of God's ideal will. Doing His will keeps you on track to your destiny and propels you into the most exciting and fulfilling adventure you can hope to experience in this world. It's a tailor-made journey leading to eternal life in Heaven. It's exciting and achievable, as long as you're listening to God's voice and following His guidance.

*How does the journey begin?*

The most critical aspect of God's amazing plan for your life is for you to accept His Son, Jesus, as your Lord and Savior. Scripture tells us that "the wages of sin is death, but the gift of God is eternal life in Christ Jesus our Lord" (Rom. 6:23-24). Sin separates human hearts from God's heart. Prophet Isaiah says, "Your iniquities have separated you from your God; your sins have hidden his face from you, so that he will not hear" (Isa. 59:2).

By dying on the cross, Jesus bridged the infinite chasm between a fallen world and a perfect heaven. He alone closes the gap between sinful human hearts and Father God's absolutely holy heart.

You'll never be good enough or do enough good deeds to earn your way into Heaven. So, why would God want to forgive your sins? Because He loves you. That's why He sent Jesus as the Savior of the world. No matter what you've done, He'll forgive you.

*No exceptions.*

God loves you just the way you are, but He also wants to free you from sin's grip so you can take charge of your destiny and find ultimate meaning in your life. Giving your heart to Jesus breaks sin's power over you and brings you into an everlasting relationship with God the Father. Sadly, I've met far too many people who aren't interested in accepting God's free gift of eternal life!

I met "Phil" when he visited my office aboard the USS Texas in the early '80s. I'll never forget our conversation.

"Sir, I need to talk to you about something."

"Go ahead."

"It's like this, Padre. I just got a call from a friend who said I'm going to be arrested."

"Why?"

"When I was stationed in D.C. a year ago, I was part of a drug ring that just got busted. The cops found out about it. I'll probably be going to prison."

"Why'd you do it?"

"I knew it was wrong—actually it was crazy—but I needed the money. I've worried about this every day since I moved to Norfolk. I'm almost glad it's finally over. Can you come with me to tell the XO? I don't want to face him alone." That day Phil was taken into custody.

I wish I could tell you that Phil, a senior Navy petty officer with over 10 years of military service, confessed his sins and invited Jesus to be his Savior before he left the ship. He didn't. His regret wasn't over breaking the law and dishonoring God, but over getting caught. Even though he was facing court-martial and a prison sentence, God would have forgiven his sins if he'd sincerely regretted the crimes he'd committed and asked for forgiveness.

*Don't let anything keep you from receiving God's complete forgiveness. Eternal life is hanging in the balance.*

## God Really Loves The World!

Jesus is God's love gift to humanity. The Bible says, "For God so loved the world that he gave his one and only Son, that whoever believes in him shall not perish but have eternal life" (John 3:16).

Yes, Jesus died for *you*, no matter what you've done in the past. God loves you so much that He sent His son, Jesus, to a cross to save you. Accepting Jesus as your Savior frees you from the penalty of sin—eternal separation from God. Heaven awaits those who turn their backs to sin and give their hearts to Jesus.

*If you haven't done so already, why not give Jesus your life so you can spend eternity with Him in Heaven!*

Once you've accepted Jesus as your Savior, the Holy Spirit takes up residence within you. Apostle Paul assures us, saying, "And if the Spirit of Him who raised Jesus from the dead is living in you, he who raised Christ from the dead will also give life to your mortal bodies through His Spirit, who lives in you" (Rom. 8:11).

The Holy Spirit empowers you to do God's will and stay on course to your destiny. When you're doing God's will, His Kingdom comes to Earth through you. Jesus tells us to pray, "Our Father in heaven, hallowed be Your name, *Your kingdom* come, *Your will be done* on earth as it is in heaven..." (Matt. 6:9-10).

Your destiny—the path to ultimate meaning—is realized in doing God's will and bringing His Kingdom to earth. Jesus preached the Kingdom gospel. His first sermon was, "*Repent of your sins and turn to God, for the Kingdom of Heaven is near*" (Matt. 4:17 NLT). Seeking His Kingdom is so critical to Jesus' plan to redeem the world that He tells us to, "*Seek the Kingdom of God above all else*" (Matt. 6:33 NLT).

Following God's plans for your life has everything to do with experiencing *ultimate* meaning in this life and after that, eternal life in Heaven. The essential element in fulfilling your destiny is doing God's will every day as He reveals it to you in ways you'll understand. It's in listening attentively to God that His plans are revealed to you day after day.

## How Does God Speak?

God speaks through the Bible, circumstances, sermons, prophecy, words of knowledge, godly counsel, in a still, small voice in your mind, and in many other ways. Discovering and taking charge of your destiny hinges on your willingness to obey what God is saying to you. Hearing without obeying will sidetrack your spiritual life. That's why Jesus says, "Therefore consider carefully how you listen. Whoever has will be given more; whoever does not have, even what he thinks he has will be taken from him" (Luke 8:18).

*Consider carefully how you listen. Your destiny hangs in the balance!*

When I was a college senior contemplating graduate school, I prayed daily for guidance. One night while I was studying, God interrupted my thoughts with a surprising sense of His presence.

He said in my heart, "*You are going to be a Navy chaplain.*" I was stunned by such a radical revelation. At the time I was a junior Naval Reserve enlisted sailor, a committed Christian for only two years, and hadn't even read the Old Testament—yet God was telling me I was going to seminary to become a minister of the Gospel and a military chaplain. Incredible!

It seemed much too grand to me. But that was His plan. Even though I couldn't imagine being a chaplain at the time, I obeyed God, contacted my faith group's chaplaincy office, and arranged an interview with the director. With his blessing, I attended seminary following graduation—an economics major amidst Bible college graduates—and God brought me through three challenging years of Greek, Hebrew, theology, and many other unfamiliar subjects.

The following year I was ordained and commissioned as a Navy chaplain and served 23 more years on active duty. It all began with hearing from and obeying God, and then stepping into my destiny.

*Don't let anything keep you from stepping into **your** destiny!*

## MAKE TIME TO LISTEN TO GOD.

Jesus teaches us to listen to God. He says, "Everyone who listens to the Father and learns from Him comes to Me" (John 6:45). He frequently spent time conversing with God. Luke tells us, "…Jesus often withdrew to lonely places and prayed" (Luke 5:16). If the Son of God prioritized conversing with Father God, every Christian should do the same.

Are you taking time to listen to Him? If not, what's stopping you? Too busy? That's all too common today, but it's really no excuse.

I now serve with the Chaplain of the U.S. Senate. Since September 2003 I've counseled Christian staffers on Capitol Hill who work 60 or more hours a week, rarely pray or read the

Bible, and wonder why they're feeling disheartened and alienated from God. They've lost control of their lives and don't know what's gone wrong. That's simple!

*They aren't listening to God!* They work hard, play hard, and give God a few leftover minutes a day.

They're robbing themselves of God's wise counsel and loving affirmation. They're missing intimate moments with the Creator of the universe because they're on a merry-go-round of constant activity that's robbing them of quiet times with God.

## How to Listen to God

Do you want to connect with God? Then slow down for a while. Turn off your television, computer, cell phone. Sit in a comfortable chair, take a few deep breaths, and relax.

As you prepare yourself to receive whatever God has for you, confess your sins and then quiet your mind. After you feel calm and collected, open your Bible and slowly read a few favorite passages aloud. Then sit silently and wait for God to speak.

Listening to God takes concentration and patience. It's hard work to slow down a busy mind and listen for His still, small voice, but well worth the effort, because listening for God is often rewarded with timely responses. I find it helpful to start my listening sessions reading Scripture aloud and then praying, "Lord, please make Your voice so clear I can't possibly miss it. I'm available for whatever You want me to do."

You'll learn to recognize His voice by spending quality time listening for Him to speak. He may whisper within your heart in subtle ways you'll miss if you aren't listening attentively. So, discipline yourself to keep listening. He'll communicate in ways you'll understand. If it's not in His still, small voice, He may communicate to you through Scripture, sermons, prayer, prophecy, other people, or circumstances.

Moses heard God speaking from a burning bush, Elijah in a still, small voice. Joseph was told in dreams to take Mary as his wife and flee with his family to Egypt. God communicated with Peter in a vision and with Paul through an angel. God certainly knows the best way for you to hear His voice.

*If you don't know already, you'll soon discover how God speaks to you.*

My wife and I often begin our morning devotions by singing praise songs, reading Scripture, and praying the concerns on our hearts. Then we wait for God to speak. Some days He has detailed instructions and on other days just a few words of affirmation.

During our 30 years in ministry, we've met people who hear God's audible voice, others who see sentences in their minds, and some who have distinct impressions about something or someone. One friend has amazing visions of Jesus, while another frequently hears His voice within her heart.

A few people have told us the Lord brings Scripture passages into their minds that meet specific needs. Others sense His love, comfort, and joy. Our daughter received confirmation to a specific prayer request in the form of affirming warmth and peace.

God will communicate with you in whatever way He knows you'll best hear Him. Your job is to be listening when He's speaking. So find a quiet place every day and listen to God. He'll get through to you.

## WHAT ARE YOU LISTENING FOR?

In listening for God, you'll eventually receive specific directions for your life. These may come from Scripture passages He brings to your mind, or from an unexpected meeting with someone who provides something you specifically requested from God. His guidance can come as a sudden burden to help someone, conviction to stop doing something or start something new, an unexpected open or closed door, or a revelation that comes in a dream, vision, prophecy, or word of knowledge.

God imparts His instructions and wisdom to those whose hearts are attentive to Him. The key to hearing God speak is taking the time to listen to Him. He'll always communicate in ways you'll understand, but He may not tell you what you want to hear!

In a recent quiet time, the Lord spoke a word into my heart when I asked Him why He wants every Christian to cultivate the discipline of listening for Him. Here's what I recorded in my journal:

*No one's life will have ultimate meaning unless he or she listens attentively to Me; so set your heart on things above. This is a day-to-day adventure. It is much like walking toward sunrise on a cloudless morning. As you continue your journey, the first hints of daybreak begin to illuminate the shadowy figures around you. The darkness loses its fearfulness as the trees and rocks around you take form.*

*The world is in darkness. Unless you listen attentively to Me, you will remain in darkness. But if you risk yourself and reach out to Me, I will illuminate your heart with love that drives out darkness and opens your eyes to the true meaning of life. That is to live moment by moment in My love. It is to experience Me and follow Me. It is to walk in the light of My Word. It is to carry My love to the world and light up the lives of those in darkness.*

*Take Charge of Your Destiny*
*Principle One:*
*Unless you listen attentively to God,*
*your life will have no ultimate meaning.*

# ACTION STEPS

## STEP ONE: MAKE TIME TO LISTEN TO GOD

To cultivate the discipline of listening to God, you have to carve out quality time for Him. You absolutely must eliminate "non-value-added" activities from your life. Evaluate your daily routine and see what time-wasters are keeping you from spending time with God. Decide what contributes to a meaningful life and what is degrading your already overloaded existence. If you want to discover your destiny and live an ultimately meaningful life, you have to take charge of your schedule and make time for God!

## STEP TWO: EXPECT GOD TO SURPRISE YOU

The Lord not only speaks to you during daily devotions; He also speaks in the midst of a busy day. He'll sometimes interrupt your routine with unexpected opportunities for Kingdom service. You could call these opportunities divine interruptions, God-incidents, or Kingdom moments.

Recently, I was boarding the subway when I noticed a tough-looking guy sitting at the end of the car. I felt drawn to sit down in front of him. A moment later, a name came into my mind, "*Daniel.*"

It was one of the few times in my life I've been given a stranger's name. I confirmed that God was speaking to me by turning around and asking the man if his name was Daniel. He said, "Yes."

I was further prompted to say, "Daniel, the Lord sent me here tonight to tell you that He loves you very much. He wants you to fulfill your destiny, but you're heading in the wrong direction, aren't you?" He nodded as tears started trickling down his cheeks. Then I encouraged him to go back to church and seek the Lord with all his heart. He told me he'd go the following Sunday.

God will employ you in Kingdom business if you're willing. So tell the Lord you're available to do His will. With your permission He'll tell you what to do and how to do it!

## CONCLUSION

If you want to fulfill your destiny and live an ultimately meaningful life, Jesus must be the center of all you are and do. There are no shortcuts to cultivating intimacy with Him, because a quality spiritual life requires a consistent investment of time in listening for Him to speak and doing what He tells you to do.

Only Jesus can reveal His best plans for your life and equip you to live your life in such a way that you find ultimate meaning in your time on earth.

I challenge you to put the action steps above into practice by making the hard decisions needed to tune in to God's voice so you will fulfill your destiny and see God's Kingdom come where you do His will.

In the next chapter, you'll learn how to recognize the devil's devious attacks, overcome temptation, and stand firm in your walk with Jesus.

### ENDNOTE

1. H.W. Smith and M.E. Dieter (1997). *The Christian's Secret of a Holy Life: The Unpublished Personal Writings of Hannah Whitall Smith* (November 30); Oak Harbor: Logos Research Systems, Inc.

# Chapter 2

# Don't Be Deceived

*Dear Friends, I warn you as temporary residents and for-
eigners to keep away from worldly desires that wage war
against your very souls. Be careful to live properly among
your unbelieving neighbors. Then even if they accuse you of
doing wrong, they will see your honorable behavior, and
they will give honor to God when He judges the world.* —
*Apostle Peter* (1 Peter 2:11-12 NLT)

*Above all else, guard your heart for it is the wellspring of
life.* —*King Solomon* (Proverbs 4:23)

The devil is a deceiver, accuser, and liar. He hates God, and
he hates you for loving God. He'll do whatever he can to divert
you from your destiny. Stay alert, because he's prowling around
like a roaring lion looking for someone to devour.

*Don't let that "someone" be you.*

The saddest words I've ever heard a fellow clergyman say
were, "I just don't know how this happened." As he sat weeping
in my office, the broken man disclosed the sordid details of an
adulterous affair that ultimately ended his military career, marriage, and ordained ministry. He perceived himself as a victim,
but he'd strayed into a forbidden zone where no helping professional has the right to go. He ignored his conscience, gave into
his passions, and ruined his life. He also forfeited his life-long
military pension.

If you're a follower of Jesus, you're a front-line soldier in God's army. Every day you're in spiritual battle—carefully planned and executed to undermine your life and steal your destiny.

The devil wants to take you out!

God's calling you to stand for what is right, good, and true in a world headed into an ignoble abyss. You're called to a holy life—one that honors God and furthers His Kingdom.

The allure of illicit relationships is one of the devil's favorite weapons against believers. Yielding to unsanctioned sexual urges will quickly and surely undermine your spiritual life, relationships, and reputation. And as a leader in your home, work place, or community, you must realize that everyone around you is bombarded by sexual images and fantasies that can lead them into very dark places.

## DON'T LET THE DEVIL TAKE YOU OUT.

A young Christian woman visited my office to discuss a personal problem. She was in her early 20s and quite fidgety as she sat across from me. She started crying when I asked her how I could help her.

She recounted a sad story of a fatherless childhood. Finally, she told me about her rocky relationship with a guy she'd been with for two years.

"I did anything for him, Sir. Anything."

"What do you mean?"

"I mean anything. Anything he asked me to do, I did."

"So why did you come to see me?"

"He hurt me last night. After all I've done for him, he hit me, told me I was a tramp, then threw me out."

We met weekly for counseling until she was able to ask God to forgive her and deal with the rejection and abuse she'd experienced. Eventually, she recovered her dignity, finished her enlistment, and enrolled in college. The sexually transmitted disease her ex-boyfriend gave her is incurable.

*All sins have consequences.*

Don't be deceived by the great deceiver! Instead, be wise to his ways and resist him at every turn. You can't embrace the world's values and expect God to bless your life. Purity may not be in vogue in secular America, but it's essential if you're committed to taking charge of your destiny and making a positive impact in this world. God demands loyalty and obedience in exchange for blessing. He's calling you to honor Him with your heart, mind, and body.

Don't slip into sexual sin. The only intimate relationships God sanctions are those within the covenant of marriage.

*No exceptions.*

Not for dating Christians, not for unhappy Christians, not for separated Christians. Why? God forbids it for your good. The spiritual union of two souls has supernatural ramifications. Within God's will, sexual union brings completion, oneness, and divine blessing. Outside God's will, it causes division, separation, and loss.

You have a much more important life to live than you may think. God's calling you to live for His glory. Your destiny hinges on your commitment to obeying God. Any sacrifice God requires of you is a small price to pay for the blessings to come. Apostle Paul says:

> *Therefore, I urge you, brothers, in view of God's mercy, to offer your bodies as living sacrifices, holy and pleasing to God—this is your spiritual act of worship. Do not conform any longer to the pattern of this world, but be transformed by the renewing of your mind. Then you will be able to test and approve what God's will is—His good, pleasing and perfect will* (Romans 12:1-2).

## WHAT'S THE BIG DEAL?

Far too often we see Christian leaders' secret sins exposed in the media. Most are married men involved in illicit sexual relationships—some with other men. Somehow they were deceived into thinking their sinful conduct wouldn't come to light. Scripture tells us that our sins always have consequences. "The Lord sees everything, and He watches us closely. Sinners are trapped and caught by their own evil deeds. They get lost and die because of their foolishness and lack of self-control" (Prov. 5:21-23 CEV).

But it's not just a few prominent leaders who are struggling with sin. We all struggle with sin. God's calling *every* believer to offer his or her body, mind, and spirit in living to please Him. Why do many Christians hold back?

*They're still captivated by sin.*

One of my fellow pastors told me that a married couple in his congregation agreed that each could engage in a chat room relationship with another person as long as neither became intimate with his or her online "friend." Within a month, the couple separated because the husband wanted more than a chat room romance with the women he'd met online.

*Don't flirt for any reason. Instead, "set your heart on things above"* (see Col. 3:1).

The danger of uncontrolled imagination (fantasy) is its power to blind you to the unintended consequences of your thought patterns and actions. A pattern of thought often becomes a behavior pattern.

Satan is very experienced in seduction. He often focuses on your thoughts because he knows that *as you think, you feel, and as you feel, you act.*

Add to the power of unbridled imagination the seductive lure of the Internet, and you could lose control of your life in seconds. The enemy wants to take you out, but he can only do it with your help. It seems that some people aren't putting up much of a fight. So what about you? Is there a problem with your inner life?

## WHERE DOES THE PROBLEM BEGIN?

In her book *The Warning Signs of Infidelity*, Nancy C. Anderson states:

> Illicit relationships often begin innocently with co-workers, but there are many avenues into an unholy relationship. One author writes, "Affairs begin in many ways and for many reasons, so we must be always on guard for the slightest hint of temptation. Because hints turn into flirtations, flirtations turn into attractions, attractions turn into affairs, and affairs turn into disasters."[1]

Everyone still sins to some degree, but that's not an excuse to stop resisting temptation. Oswald Chambers says, "If the world, the flesh, and the devil have knocked you out once, get up and face them again, and again, until you have done with them."[2]

If you sincerely desire to break free from the sins that easily entangle you and rob you of intimacy with the Lord, He will strengthen you for the battle.

But you have a big part in your personal battle for purity. Keep fighting no matter what happens. You can't quit fighting if you fall. So if you fall, don't remain in defeat; get up, repent, and keep going. As the writer of Proverbs says:

> *The godly may trip seven times, but they will get up again* (Proverbs 24:16 NLT).

## WHAT CONTROLS YOUR THOUGHTS?

Ongoing victory hinges on what controls your thoughts. As I stated earlier, what you allow into your mind often becomes a pattern of thought that eventually leads to a pattern of behavior. *As you think, you feel and as you feel, you act.*

What you allow to control your mind has a powerful impact on your thoughts, feelings, *and* actions. If you read horror novels before bed, your dreams will most likely be impacted—even to the point that you develop disturbing nightmares.

If you read automobile magazines, you could be tempted to trade a perfectly good car for a sleeker, faster, more expensive model. It only follows that if you allow romantic fantasies to linger in your mind, you'll excite your libido. The more you feed your flesh, the more it controls your thoughts. Much like a drug addict who needs progressively more drugs to get high, you can become addicted to a variety of things that degrade your walk with God, including lust.

I've counseled hundreds of men and women who were struggling with their thought lives. During a long deployment at sea, one of my fellow officers was obsessing about sex every time I saw him. I tried to tell him he was in for a big fall if he gave in to his sick desires. He reacted angrily and told me to mind my own business. After visiting a house of ill repute in a foreign country, he developed a painful sexually transmitted disease—so debilitating he could barely walk to the bathroom. A week later, I asked him if he thought it was worth it; his crude reply was, "He– no, and I'm not going to do it again!"

After the fact, it didn't take much for him to see his mistake. Why didn't he anticipate the negative consequences of his actions? He was blinded by lust!

Most Christians are dedicated to honoring God with their lives and have no desire to fall from His grace. Yet every one of us is tainted in some way by our culture and its eroding values that have invaded our schools, homes, businesses, and churches.

In the '80s, my family and I lived in Japan. We had only one "family friendly" English television channel in our apartment. When we returned to the States after three years, we were shocked by noticeably more sexually suggestive and anti-Christian programming. It took an extended absence to notice a significant change in our cultural values. I'm afraid our national awareness of the continuing moral decline is much like the frog in the kettle that is eventually scalded because it didn't notice the gradual increase in temperature until it was too late to escape.

Billy Graham said years ago, "I'm shocked by what doesn't shock me anymore."

*What doesn't shock you anymore?*

## DON'T BE DECEIVED.

Discontent is a root cause of moral failure. Its genesis—deep within the human heart—takes the form of nagging emptiness and longing for connection to something or someone beyond us. Its power can be dark, even frightening. You may feel at times like you're caught in a swirling eddy, unable to fight the force pulling you under.

All this is permitted and measured by our loving God who says through apostle Paul:

> *No temptation has seized you except what is common to man. And God is faithful; he will not let you be tempted beyond what you can bear. But when you are tempted, he will also provide a way out so that you can stand up under it* (1 Corinthians 10:13).

Even in the darkest times, God's light is present. You may not feel Him with you, but He's there. Nothing can hide His light. You don't have to yield to temptation in a quest to ease your pain or loneliness—His power is available to you in your weakness. Cry out to God for help!

But why should you feel discontented in the first place? After all, you're redeemed, filled with the Holy Spirit, and destined for eternity. Why don't your religious observances always bring you peace of heart and power over your worldly cravings?

You may be a victim of spiritual deception. Perhaps you've been duped into thinking you can live on the edge and still walk in unwavering righteousness. If so, you have a serious "heart" problem to resolve.

Your heart is the center of life and thought. King David asks:

> *Who may ascend the hill of the Lord? Who may stand in His holy place?*

He replies:

> *He who has clean hands and a **pure heart**.* (See Psalm 24:3-4.)

Your heart is the core of your being and the meeting place of eternity and mortality. It's where the spark of life resides, where the longing for eternity is centered, and where the hope of union with God exists as an unquenchable desire until it finds its fulfillment in Him. You'll hear God clearly as long as your heart is pure.

That's why the enemy tempts you to sin. He wants to keep you from hearing God's voice and fulfilling your destiny. He doesn't care how you fall, just that you fall into temptation.

*So how do you avoid an unanticipated fall?*

By taking charge of your destiny and waging war against the evil one who works continually to take your eyes off of Jesus and tempt you to sin.

While I was journaling one morning, the Lord shared the following insights about spiritual warfare:

> *The enemy of your soul seeks to dishonor Me by causing you to focus on the flesh and not live in the Spirit. Immediate gratification rarely brings lasting peace and joy. But making the hard choices now brings reward—lasting reward—later. Those with a penchant for self-destruction*

*often sow the seeds of their own downfall in the little com-*
*promises they make early in life. Once a pattern of disobe-*
*dience is established, the gradual slide into great sin is*
*inevitable. It takes just a few unrepentant actions to cause*
*the heart to gradually cool and then become cold to Me.*

*The world is very cold. There is little lasting satisfaction in*
*sin, so rebellion must increase and become more pro-*
*nounced if any satisfaction is to be found. Once sin is an*
*established pattern, the enemy feeds it with dark ideas and*
*longings. Sin becomes abomination if it is left unchecked.*
*The slide toward complete yielding to darkness comes when*
*My voice is ignored and My word shunned.*

*My people, won't you examine your hearts and see what is*
*there? Can't you recognize the rebellion in your hearts*
*manifested in sinful thoughts, actions, and attitudes?*

*Take Charge of Your Destiny*
*Principle Two:*
*Fix your eyes on Jesus and you will avoid moral failure.*

## A CTION  S TEPS

### S TEP  O NE:  R ESIST  T EMPTATION.

Does the devil really make us sin, as some espouse? Hardly! We give in to temptation because we want to. James tells us:

*When tempted, no one should say, "God is tempting me." For God cannot be tempted by evil, nor does he tempt any-one;* **but each one is tempted when, by his own evil desire, he is dragged away and enticed.** *Then, after desire has conceived, it gives birth to sin; and sin, when it is full-grown, gives birth to death* (James 1:13-15).

So what's James talking about? You're tempted by your own evil desires, dragged away, and enticed. Then after your desires are conceived, they give birth to sin that can lead to death. The enemy's flaming darts only "hit home" in unsanctified areas of your heart, and you only fall into sin because you don't try to escape.

Take heart, because there's always an escape route, as Paul tells us in First Corinthians 10:13. Please memorize this passage! It could save you from making a *big* mistake.

Moral compromise is often gradual. It's failure in little things that gives way to bigger things. The enemy is very patient in relentlessly pursing God's children. He whispers far more often than he roars. He flirts around the edges of your conscience and twists God's words. "Did God really say...?" he asks. King David fell into sexual sin because he failed to take control of his thoughts. Once his thoughts turned from God to self-gratification, David quickly started a chain of events culminating in an out-of-wedlock pregnancy and the death of a faithful and loyal man of integrity—Uriah the Hittite, the husband of Bathsheba. (See Second Samuel 11.)

You have to catch yourself early, avert your gaze quickly, and run away from temptation. Paul says to "flee from sexual immorality. All other sins a man commits are outside his body, but he who sins sexually sins against his own body" (1 Cor. 6:18). The book of Hebrews also has advice for those struggling with any type of temptation:

> *Therefore, since we have a great high priest who has gone through the heavens, Jesus the Son of God, let us hold firmly to the faith we profess. For we do not have a high priest who is unable to sympathize with our weaknesses, but we have one who has been tempted in every way, just as we are—yet was without sin.* **Let us then approach the throne of grace with confidence, so that we may receive mercy and find grace to help us in our time of need** (Hebrews 4:14-16).

Remember that when you fix your eyes on Jesus you will avoid moral failure. So, take Paul's advice and run as fast as you can when you're tempted. You have too much to lose if you don't!

### STEP TWO: AVOID THE NEAR OCCASION OF SIN.

Moral failure—adultery and all other sexual sins; every breach of integrity; every selfish act of immoral behavior or sinfulness—is rooted in rebellion of the heart. Selfishness is a form of idolatry—appeasing selfish desires over valuing another. It's rooted in the dark, unsanctified areas of your heart.

So, beware of what excites you. You know if you have an obsession and could soon fall when your thoughts continually drift to food, lust, money, power, revenge, jealousy, and similar things. Do you have any area in your life where the devil has a foothold and causes you embarrassment? If so, confess it as sin, repent, renounce the behavior, and ask God to help you resist it in the future.

Remember: the enemy can only take you out with your cooperation. So fight back by taking control of your thoughts.

That's why Paul says:

> ...*whatever is true, whatever is noble, whatever is right, whatever is pure, whatever is lovely, whatever is admirable—if anything is excellent or praiseworthy—* **think about such things** *(Philippians 4:8).*

When you yield to temptation, you empower the devil by giving him a foothold in your heart and mind. The more you yield to sinful thoughts and actions, the more power sin gains over you.

The opposite is also true. If you resist the tempter, you take away his footholds in your thoughts. James says:

> *Submit yourselves, then, to God.* **Resist the devil, and he will flee from you.** *Come near to God and He will come near to you. Wash your hands, you sinners, and purify your hearts, you double-minded....Humble yourselves before the Lord, and He will lift you up (James 4:7-8,10).*

It's important to remember that those who fall into moral failure often experience disastrous consequences as a result of their indiscretions: public embarrassment, divorce, dismissal from a ministry, financial setbacks, loneliness, self-hatred, rebellious children, even suicide. "The thief comes only to steal and kill and destroy" (John 10:10). The devil can only "get you" if you don't resist him in God's power. So resist him! Tell him to go back to where he came from, in Jesus' mighty name!

Without elaboration, let me give you a short "to do" list to help you guard your heart and mind as well as resist the enemy when he attacks:

- Don't expose yourself to immoral music, DVDs, movies, or websites.

- Cancel cable TV if you're lured to channels that would embarrass Jesus.

- Find an accountability partner and pray together weekly.

- Recognize and renounce destructive thought patterns.

- Meditate on and memorize helpful Scripture passages.

- Daily confess all known sins and ask the Holy Spirit to fill you with His power.

- Ask your pastor for counseling if you're unable to break sinful thought or behavior patterns.

## CONCLUSION

Jesus is your North Star, your bearing mark. He's the standard by which all else is judged. If you fix your eyes on Him, you'll avoid moral failure, fulfill your destiny, and honor God. Live to please God. Living to please Him frees you from looking to the world for gratification and affirmation.

The world's enticements often lead to bondage; Jesus always leads you to freedom. That's what He means when He says, "If you hold to My teaching, you are really My disciples. Then you will know the truth, and the truth will set you free" (John 8:31-32).

Humankind's relentless pursuit of pleasure yields nothing of ultimate value. It's only in deep spiritual union with God that you'll discover true meaning and deep satisfaction in this life.

Once you unreservedly commit yourself to Him, a vision of His Kingdom, power, and glory will fill your heart.

Knowing God intimately makes worldly pleasures pale by comparison. To know God as Father, Son, and Holy Spirit is to experience the deepest possible fulfillment and most rewarding destiny.

In the next chapter, you'll learn how doing things God's way keeps you on course to your destiny and brings you great joy and peace every day.

### ENDNOTES

1. Nancy C. Anderson, *The Warning Signs of Infidelity*, Growthtrac.com.

2. *Draper's Quotes*, 1,024.

CHAPTER 3

# Live God's Way

*Good and upright is the Lord; therefore He instructs sinners in His ways. He guides the humble in what is right and teaches them His way.* —*King David* (Psalm 25:8-9).

"I want what God wants, that's why I am so merry." —Saint Francis of Assisi (A.D. 1181–1226)

God's ways are *always* best. No exceptions. Why? He always has your destiny in mind. Your absolutely best life is found in the center of His ideal will.

As a junior chaplain stationed in Norfolk, Virginia, I visited a sailor in the city jail. "Jimmy" was 22, in his second year of marriage, and having terrible financial problems. Seeing no other way out of debt, he robbed a grocery store and was arrested ten minutes after he fled with a few hundred dollars. The surprisingly polite and mild-mannered young man was facing decades of incarceration.

The saddest part of the story came just before I left. "Chaplain, the crazy thing is that my wife was praying for God to bring us money, but I knew that wouldn't happen. The day after I was busted my wife got a check from her uncle that covered all our bills."

Chuck Swindoll is absolutely right in saying, "Our adversary is a master strategist, forever fogging up our minds with smokescreens."[1]

Jimmy learned that truth the hard way.

## DEVELOP PATIENT ENDURANCE.

Impatience and lack of faith in God's unfailing love often drive us to premature action. If we just wait patiently, God will show us His way. Yet three decades of ministry have proven to me that most people aren't willing to wait for God to reveal His will. The sad truth is...

*Impatience often leads to pain.*

The Psalmist tells us to "be still before the Lord and wait patiently for Him; do not fret when men succeed in their ways..." (Ps. 37:7). The Lord honors us when we wait for Him to reveal His ways and stop fretting about what we can't control. Take this to heart,

*Living in tune with the Holy Spirit sensitizes you to God's ways.*

The devil wants you to think there are no solutions to what may appear from your vantage point as unsolvable problems. Moses may have been tempted to feel that way with an enemy army quickly approaching and a vast sea in front of him. Shadrach, Meshach, and Abednego may have felt that way when they were cast into a fiery furnace. Elderly Daniel may have been similarly tempted when he was dropped into a den of lions. But these heroes of faith didn't let the seemingly impossible cause them to fear or compromise their integrity. They were committed to doing things God's way no matter what it cost—even if it cost their lives.

## THERE'S GREAT BLESSING IN LIVING GOD'S WAY.

God has good news for you: He's able to do far more than you can ever ask or imagine (see Eph. 3:20).

Moses witnessed the Red Sea parting and the Egyptian army drowning. (See Exodus chapter 14.)

Shadrach, Meshach, and Abednego not only survived their fiery ordeal, but they also met one "like a son of the gods" in the furnace and escaped unharmed (see Dan. 3:25).

Daniel spent a night with ferocious beasts but testified the next morning that an angel closed their mouths (see Dan. 6:21).

You need to accept this truth: If you live life your way—within the limitations of your intellect, physical prowess, persuasive personality, and life experiences—you'll miss your destiny without even realizing you've been duped.

Our heavenly Father offers you His way to a meaningful life.

Obedience isn't optional, but God won't force you to obey Him.

It's only in living God's way, in God's power, for God's glory that you'll surpass the limits of your lower nature and fulfill your destiny.

## MAKE WISE DECISIONS

You can't have your way and God's way at the same time. If you're wise, you'll accept God's will as your own and commit yourself to advancing His Kingdom. At first it may seem risky to ask God to direct your life, but the blessings that follow your obedience will confirm how wise it is to live God's way.

As a teen I wanted a motorcycle. For months I longed for the open roads and owning my own wheels. When I told my dad I was planning to use my savings to purchase my dream bike—one I just couldn't live without—he just smiled quietly and stared at me.

After a few silent moments I was squirming. Then he said, "Son, you can't buy a motorcycle if you want to live in this house." It was his way of telling me that buying a motorcycle was a dumb idea.

I stormed off to sulk. After calming down, I realized he was right—we lived where winter lasted six months. I'd have no transportation when I needed it most. My dad loved me and wanted the best for me. He saw the flaw in my plan even when I was blind to it.

He bought me an old used car, but it had heat!

Our loving heavenly Father sees every flaw in your self-made plans and every blessing you'll experience in living His way by following His carefully crafted plans for your life.

He'll allow you to do your own thing—even if you choose to sin.

But eventually you'll discover that His ways are always best.

I've found that it's worth whatever it appears to cost me in the short run to remain in the center of God's will in the long run. I think you'll discover the same truth. That's because,

*You were created to love God **and** do His will.*

John says:

*But if anyone obeys His word, God's love is truly made complete in him. This is how we know we are in Him: Whoever claims to live in Him must walk as Jesus did* (1 John 2:5-6).

Jesus lived to honor His Father.

If you really love Jesus, you'll do the things Jesus did as the Holy Spirit leads you day to day. In living like Jesus, you'll also see God's Kingdom come where His will is done.

*So do what God tells you to do and don't worry; you aren't alone in the battle.*

God's will is so important that He'll do whatever it takes to help you succeed in what you're called to do. He wants you to live His way by allowing Him to guide you day by day. It's to those who commit to doing things His way that He entrusts the most important missions.

The Lord desires for you to live in His will. I believe the Lord is asking us:

*How can I entrust the sacred message of the Gospel to those with filthy hands and hearts? It is a pearl of great price, not a cheap imitation. It is life and liberty, yet many take a nibble and are satisfied when the whole feast awaits them. Don't let the distractions of this world rob you of your birthright. Don't let the meager offerings of a carnal existence distract you from your destiny. You are My child, and I will bless your obedience with good things. If you are willing and obedient, you will certainly experience My blessings. If you rebel and disobey, I will withhold My blessings and let you suffer the consequences of your sin. Choose life. Choose Me.*

## How God's Kingdom Is Established

God's Kingdom is established where His will is done. It comes as He releases His power into the natural world through you as you do His will.

He knows exactly what He needs you to do, and He's looking for you to cooperate with His plans in establishing His Kingdom in the hearts of those around you.

*It's time to step out in obedience and reclaim the territory that is rightly yours.*

Pastor Bill Johnson tells us:

We were born to rule—rule over creation, over darkness—to plunder hell and establish the rule of Jesus wherever we go by preaching the Gospel of the Kingdom. *Kingdom* means: *King's domain.* In the original purpose of God, humankind ruled over creation. Now that sin has entered the world, creation has been infected by darkness, namely: disease, sickness, afflicting spirits, poverty, natural disasters, demonic influence, etc. Our rule is still over creation, but now it is focused on exposing and undoing the works of the devil....If I truly receive power from an encounter with the God of power, I am equipped to give it away. The invasion of God into impossible situations comes through a people who have received power from on high and learn to release it into the circumstances of life.[2]

The Lord needs your help in bringing His Kingdom to earth—a job He could have chosen to do Himself. Instead, He's delegated the responsibility to His Church and is now mobilizing a great army of motivated and consecrated believers. He's recruiting those who are ready to fulfill their destiny. He's seeking those who will do their very best in obeying Him, working in the Holy Spirit's anointing, and following His leading in establishing His Kingdom.

I believe you're reading this book because God wants you to bring His Kingdom into the lives of those you love.

## How God Prepares Us To Follow His Ways

Sanctification, surrender to God's will, and brokenness are critical to a vibrant Christian life and the establishment of God's Kingdom. That's because sanctification brings holiness, surrender brings willingness, and brokenness brings effectiveness.

The purposes of sanctification and surrender to God's will are probably obvious to you, so let me take a few moments to discuss the purpose of brokenness that is not widely taught in Western churches.

Brokenness is God's way of getting you off the throne of your life so He may rule in your heart. How does brokenness contribute to effective Christian service? Chinese theologian Watchman Nee tells us:

> Among all the people in the world, some have the Lord's life within them. Among those who have the Lord's life, we find two different kinds of conditions. With the first, the life is bound, surrounded, and locked up. With the second, the Lord has opened up a way and the life can be released. The problem with us today is not how we can have life, but how we can allow this life to flow out of us. When we say that the Lord has to break us, this is not a figure of speech or a doctrine. Our very being has to be broken by the Lord. The Lord's life is well able to spread over the whole earth. However, it is locked up within us! The Lord is well able to bless the church, yet His life is imprisoned, contained, and blocked in us! If the outer man is not broken, we can never become a blessing to the church, nor can we expect the world to receive God's grace through us![3]

I experienced brokenness as a mission pastor prior to military chaplaincy. I look back on a very cold January 1980 as the worst and best month of my life.

I was so low I wanted to leave the ministry. Nine months of nonstop effort was reaping no noticeable fruit in the lives of those I was serving. I was completely isolated, nearing burnout, and desperate for God's help.

As I knelt in our tiny living room, weeping for the first time in decades, the smothering darkness within me felt like frigid North Atlantic fog. I cried out to the Lord, "Father, I can't do this on my own. Nothing's working. My sermons are flat, no one's coming to my Sunday school class, and they aren't excited about Jesus...I'm so sorry, Father...I don't know what to do…I give up doing things my way. Just show me what to do, Father, and I'll do it."

As I surrendered my life to God's purposes, the darkness in my soul slowly gave way to an indescribable infilling. I was set free from my fear of failure and bondage of living to please others. I felt my heavenly Father's love and power pour into my heart. He healed me, empowered me, and set me on course toward my destiny.

From that day on I haven't lost the fire God poured into my heart and have only seen my burning desire for Him and His Kingdom grow hotter over the decades. Brokenness, though painful, is often God's most effective way of bringing us into great spiritual blessing. It was in my case.

God's calling you to choose His ways over your ways—to prayerfully seek His plans and fulfill them. He's looking for a radical church, a fearless church, a loving church, a serving church, a powerfully anointed church. His Kingdom comes where His will is done. Choose to live God's way, and you will fulfill your destiny.

*Take Charge of Your Destiny*
*Principle Three:*
*You can't have your way and God's way at the same time.*

## ACTION STEPS

### STEP ONE: PRAY DAILY FOR WISDOM AND POWER.

You need wisdom. As brilliant as you may be in some areas, there are still many things you don't know. Only God knows all the answers to life's questions. Solomon understood this as he was writing Proverbs. As the wisest man who ever lived, even he needed God's wisdom. That's why he tells his own son (and you) in Proverbs 2:1-6:

> *My son, if you accept my words and store up my commands within you, turning your ear to wisdom and applying your heart to understanding, and if you call out for insight and cry aloud for understanding, and if you look for it as for silver and search for it as for hidden treasure, then you will understand the fear of the Lord and find the knowledge of God. For the Lord gives wisdom, and from his mouth come knowledge and understanding.*

God's saying, "Accept My words, store up My commands, turn your ear to My wisdom, apply your heart to My understanding, call out for My insight, cry aloud for My understanding, look for it like you're searching for precious metal and hidden treasure." Then—and not before—you will understand the richness of fearing or revering God and receive the knowledge He alone can give you.

Wisdom comes from God's mind into your mind. James 1:5 says it succinctly, "If any of you need wisdom, you should ask God, and it will be given to you. God is generous and won't correct you for asking" (CEV).

Not only do you need God's wisdom to understand His ways, but you also need the power of the Holy Spirit to live God's way. Human wisdom isn't enough to bring His Kingdom to earth, and human power isn't enough to overcome the enemy's strongholds. You need God's power! That's the power Jesus commanded His disciples to wait for when He bid them farewell in Acts 1:8, "But you will receive power [*dunamis*] when the Holy Spirit comes on you; and you will be my witnesses in Jerusalem, and in all Judea and Samaria, and to the ends of the earth."

Ask God to give you His power to resist sin and walk in His ways.

## STEP TWO: READ AND STUDY GOD'S WORD.

The Bible is God's gift to the world. It contains pure truth that renews your mind and aligns your heart with God's will and ways. Understanding the relationship-degrading power of sin, King David poses an important question, "How can a young man keep his way pure?" (Ps. 119:9). He offers us his prayerful response to the Lord.

> *By living according to Your word. I seek You with all my heart; do not let me stray from Your commands. I have hidden Your word in my heart that I might not sin against You. Praise be to You, O Lord; teach me Your decrees. With my lips I recount all the laws that come from Your mouth. I rejoice in following Your statutes as one rejoices in great riches. I meditate on Your precepts and consider Your ways. I delight in your decrees; I will not neglect Your word* (Psalm 119:9-16).

Jesus teaches by example that the Word of God is, as Paul says, the sword of the Spirit—a powerful spiritual weapon. During his wilderness trial, Jesus battled the tempter with God's Word, demonstrated the importance of memorizing Scripture, and showed us the effectiveness of speaking it aloud (see Matt. 4:1-10). Like our Master, you'll face trials and temptations. Your daily dose of God's Word will prepare you for whatever the enemy sends your way.

It's critical to allow the Word of God to dwell in your heart and open your mind to God's ways. Systematic Bible study brings you to a new level of spirituality and intimacy with God.

I teach a simple, three-pronged method for learning God's Word—**Read, Study, and Pray:**

1.  Read a few chapters a day.

2.  Study a section of a chapter in depth every day.

3.  Pray about one verse during the day.

God's Word has supernatural power. It builds faith and directs you in His ways. Consistent immersion in the Word equips you for victory and keeps you on course to your destiny.

### Step Three: Commit to Living God's Way.

God knows your needs. He even knows of needs you may not be aware of. Needs that are so deep they are hidden from your recollection and reflection. Needs that can control your outlook on life and distract you from living God's way.

He desires to free you from inner torment, deep wounds, and debilitating attitudes. Your heart is the wellspring of life, but the tempter sometimes lurks in the shadowy places in your heart because he's established strongholds in your thoughts and seeks to rob you of your destiny.

Our loving heavenly Father is calling you to release your life to Him. He's calling you to yield your heart, mind, and strength. That's because He desires to equip you for spiritual battle and empower you for victory. He'll even set you free from needless toil and striving. You can rest assured that doing things God's way will bring you much more joy, peace, and fulfillment than doing your own will apart from God.

Recommit to doing things God's way by praying as King David did, "Show me your ways, O Lord, teach me your paths; guide me in your truth and teach me, for you are God my Savior, and my hope is in you all day long" (Ps. 25:4-5).

## Conclusion

Your life matters, and *you* really matter to God! After all, God created you to experience the joy of His presence and blessings. His ways will lead you to places of fulfillment and destiny. The enemy's deceptions are intended to thwart God's eternal purposes and lull you into believing your life has no purpose beyond enjoying the things of this world. That's a lie! The Lord will not force you to seek His plans to prosper you, but He'll reward you if you earnestly seek Him.

So follow the path to a meaningful life. Commit to living God's way and remember that:

> *"In the way of righteousness there is life; along that path is immortality"* (Proverbs 12:28).

In the next chapter you'll learn how to use your God-given power and authority to resist and overcome the enemy's assaults on behalf of your family, church, business, and community.

### Endnotes

1. *Draper's Quotes*, 2,260.

2. Bill Johnson, *When Heaven Invades Earth: A Practical Guide to a Life of Miracles* (Shippensburg, PA: Destiny Image, 2003), 32-33.

3. Watchman Nee, *The Breaking of the Outer Man and the Release of the Spirit* (Anaheim, CA: Living Stream Ministry, 1997), 9.

# Chapter 4

# Use Your Authority

*I saw Satan fall like lightning from heaven. I have given you authority to trample on snakes and scorpions and to overcome all the power of the enemy; nothing will harm you. However, do not rejoice that the spirits submit to you, but rejoice that your names are written in heaven. —Jesus Christ (Luke 10:18-20)*

Since only the white light of Calvary's power can dissipate the black workings of hell, the only people who can change bleak circumstances and reverse the tide of encroaching evil wherever it rises are those who pray in Jesus' name.[1] —Jack Hayford

The devil is a thief and murderer. He's a liar and the father of lies—devious, conniving, and vengeful. He's looking for easy targets. Don't let him take you out. You have too much to lose.

Cathy joined a satanic coven when she was sixteen.

She split from the group after three years and eventually gave her life to Jesus. Ten years later she and her husband started attending our home Bible study. One night the Lord led me to pray for her.

She consented, and five of us gathered around her, praying quietly. A few minutes later, I had a vision of a young girl with brown hair lying on a bed and covered with black sheets. A dark cloud hovered above her. To the side of the room there were two black candles glowing on a small altar draped in black.

I asked Cathy what this meant to her. She said I had described her old bedroom and that she, a blond, was a natural brunette. She cried as she recounted her three years in the coven and daily suicidal thoughts.

As we were praying to free her from the dark powers afflicting her, she grabbed her right ear and said she heard a loud whistle along with feeling sharp pain. After a few minutes, she experienced complete relief. We felt moved to continue praying for twenty more minutes. When we finished, Cathy was glowing. She was filled with the Holy Spirit and felt peace for the first time in over a decade.

She and her husband transferred to another city just a few days after we prayed for her.

Three months later, I was on temporary assignment in the city where Cathy and her husband had settled. They invited me to dinner, excited to tell me what had happened after the night we prayed.

Cathy was ecstatic—for three months she hadn't had a suicidal thought and was thrilled to have fallen in love with Jesus. Her husband, who hadn't known about her occult membership, was also transformed after seeing her metamorphosis.

*Every Christian on Earth has God-given spiritual power and authority. Unfortunately, most don't know how to use it!*

You may not know or believe you have it, but you do. It's time for you to understand and use your God-given authority!

Why? Because Father God is mobilizing a worldwide army of spiritual warriors dedicated to reclaiming territory that is rightfully ours. That's how His Kingdom comes to Earth.

### WHAT DO WE KNOW ABOUT THE DEVIL'S POWER AND AUTHORITY?

We face an enemy with thousands of years of experience controlling human hearts and warring against the saints. The good news is—we're on the winning team! Jesus, by dying on the cross, has already won the war for us. There are still many skirmishes to fight before Jesus returns, but ultimately the devil will meet his much-deserved end.

Apostle John tells us prophetically:

*And the devil, who deceived them, was thrown into the lake of burning sulfur, where the beast and the false prophet had been thrown. They will be tormented day and night for ever and ever* (Revelation 20:10).

A few years ago I dreamed I was outside walking on a dirt road bordering a field in which a group of men were setting up temporary fences in preparation for a construction project. As I walked along, I was approached by an overweight man who I somehow realized was planning to take my money.

He wasn't especially threatening to look at. He came up to me and pulled out a thick wallet with many pockets. He fumbled through a few of the pockets and finally found a tiny razor blade—old and dull—that was the weapon he was going to use to rob me. I told him to go away—that he had no power over me. I rebuked him in Jesus' name and then he turned and left. I continued on my journey.

I woke up and started journaling my dream. That's when the Holy Spirit told me: "The devil doesn't have any power over you that you can't overcome with the authority of Christ."

*That's really good news!*

But the bad news is that the devil's wallet was full of cash. His "wad" of cash symbolizes what people have yielded to him thinking he has the power to take it from them. That's a shame, because the devil has absolutely no authority to rob God's sons and daughters.

He's a puffed-up egomaniac whose chief aims are to rob God of glory and His children of their destiny. Compared to God's infinite power and greatness, the devil is relatively powerless. He chose the low road of rebellion and disobedience rather than the high road of obedience and blessing. He can't rob you unless you let him.

## JESUS MINISTERED IN GOD'S POWER AND AUTHORITY.

Make no mistake—Jesus never lost His divine authority as the Son of God. He didn't come to earth to win back what He still had. He came to forgive our sins and win back the delegated authority Adam and Eve relinquished to a rebellious fallen angel.

Most importantly Jesus came to redeem us from the power of sin and death. It may seem amazing to you that Jesus left His glory in Heaven when He came to earth. But our Savior had to do that to win back our authority. Paul says that Jesus,

> ...being in very nature God, did not consider equality with God something to be grasped, but made Himself nothing, taking the very nature of a servant, being made in human likeness. And being found in appearance as a man, He humbled Himself and became obedient to death—even death on a cross! (Philippians 2:6-8)

Scripture tells us that Jesus received the power of the Holy Spirit at His baptism. Why would the Son of God need to receive the Holy Spirit when He Himself is a member of the Godhead? That's because He emptied himself of His own power and glory by humbling himself to do God's will in the same way He expects His followers to do it—in the power of the Holy Spirit. Luke writes:

*When all the people were being baptized, Jesus was baptized too. And as He was praying, heaven was opened and the Holy Spirit descended on Him in bodily form like a dove. And a voice came from heaven: "You are My Son, whom I love; with You I am well pleased"* (Luke 3:21-22).

In the power of the Holy Spirit, Jesus used His authority to change water into wine, heal lepers, open blind eyes, and regenerate useless legs. He cast out demons, raised the dead, multiplied loaves and fish to feed multitudes, calmed a storm, and walked on water.

Jesus' contemporaries recognized the authority and power with which He preached the Gospel of the Kingdom, healed the sick, and delivered the demonized.

*"Be quiet!" Jesus said sternly. "Come out of him!" Then the demon threw the man down before them all and came out without injuring him.* **All the people were amazed and said to each other, "What is this teaching? With authority and power He gives orders to evil spirits and they come out!"** *And the news about Him spread throughout the surrounding area* (Luke 4:35-37).

## JESUS TELLS US TO USE OUR GOD-GIVEN AUTHORITY AND POWER.

Following His death and resurrection, Jesus told His disciples:

**All authority in heaven and on earth has been given to Me. Therefore go and make disciples of all nations,** *baptizing them in the name of the Father and of the Son and of the Holy Spirit, and teaching them to obey everything I have commanded you. And surely I am with you always, to the very end of the age* (Matthew 28:18-20).

Did you get it? *All authority in heaven* (which Jesus never lost) *and on earth* (which He won back from the devil by shedding His blood for us on the cross) has been given to Jesus. And He freely delegates that authority to you. Not because you earned it, but because it is available to every Christian on earth to extend the boundaries of God's Kingdom.

*And there's a bonus.*

Not only do you have delegated authority (*exousia*), you've also been granted the power (*dunamis*) to exercise it in doing God's will. Jesus says, "I have given you **authority** to trample on snakes and scorpions and to overcome all the **power** of the enemy; nothing will harm you" (Luke 10:19).

The book of Acts is filled with accounts of deliverance, healings, and other miracles. History also records miracles through the ages. Around the world today, Christians are seeing God moving in the miraculous.

Our daughter recently returned from a mission trip to Brazil. She and two other ladies were asked to pray for a woman with a cancerous breast tumor. Their translator happened to be a nurse who described the size and location of the tumor. As the ladies were praying, the tumor began to shrink.

Each time the nurse examined the affected area, the tumor was smaller, until after 45 minutes of prayer, it completely disappeared.

The reality of total health in Heaven invaded the aberrant reality of cancer in a human body. As the Holy Spirit moved in power, Heaven's reality replaced sickness with health. You have all the power and authority you need to do whatever God calls you to do. The devil can't overcome you if you know how to use God's delegated power and authority. Paul tells us:

> *Finally, be strong in the Lord and in His mighty power. Put on the full armor of God so that you can take your stand against the devil's schemes. For our struggle is not against*

*flesh and blood, but against the rulers, against the author-*
*ities, against the powers of this dark world and against the*
*spiritual forces of evil in the heavenly realms. Therefore put*
*on the full armor of God, so that when the day of evil*
*comes, you may be able to stand your ground, and after*
*you have done everything, to stand* (Ephesians 6:10-13).

## GOD WILL EMPOWER YOU FOR KINGDOM SERVICE.

If you want to see God's Kingdom come where you do His
will, you'll need His power to effectively share the Gospel, heal
the sick, and free the demonized. You must also learn how to
flow with the moves of God and work in the gifts of the Holy
Spirit.

Holy Spirit baptism is God's impartation of supernatural
power. Every Christian has the Holy Spirit resident in him or
her when he or she yields his or her life to Jesus Christ as his or
her Lord and Savior. That's why Paul asks:

*Do you not know that your body is a temple of the Holy*
*Spirit, who is in you, whom you have received from God?*
(1 Corinthians 6:19)

But the Holy Spirit doesn't have every Christian at His
disposal. It's as if some are sitting on the bench and the coach
wants to put them in the ballgame, but they've left their uni-
forms, bats, and gloves in the locker room. They could go out on
the field, but they'd be only minimally effective.

Without the Holy Spirit's power, you're not fully equipped
to do the work God is calling you to do. Your power is too limited. God's power is unlimited.

John the Baptist says of Jesus, "I baptize you with water,
but he will baptize you with the Holy Spirit!" (Mark 1:8). The
Holy Spirit equips Christians for effective Kingdom service. He
releases a mighty river of supernatural power into the natural

world by working through those who are doing God's will. Through our obedient service, we overcome the enemy and bring God's Kingdom to earth. Where God's Kingdom comes, sin and sickness have no place.

When we prayed for Cathy and commanded the demons harassing her mind to flee, the Kingdom reality of Heaven became the reality in her life. She was set free from the devil's grip. Why? Darkness can't stand the light of God's Spirit, so the demons fled when the Holy Spirit was released into her through the laying on of hands and the declaration of the Word of God. Her heart was reclaimed and her mind and emotions restored to wholeness. We just asserted God's delegated authority as His representatives on earth, and the demons had to flee. How did that happen?

Kingdom power invaded Cathy's inner being, purging it of the darkness she had allowed to enter her through occult involvement, and filling her with God's light and love. The Kingdom of light and love always trumps the kingdom of darkness. Myles Monroe tells us:

> God reigns as King and absolute Sovereign over all things in both the spiritual and physical realms. After He created the earth with its varied plant and animal life, He created humankind to rule over the earthly domain. God is King of the universe, and we are His ruling representatives in the physical realm. The earth is our designated territory. As God's vice-regents in this world, *we are the Kingdom of God on earth.* The Kingdom of God, therefore, is not the earth itself, but the ones chosen to function as His rulers in the earthly domain. This planet is not the Kingdom of God; God's Kingdom is us carrying out His dominion on this planet. God's Kingdom is manifest in His people rather than in a particular place.[2]

Every day we're drawing nearer to the culmination of time. Jesus has won the battle, and the devil knows his days are limited. The evil one is like a drunk reeling from too much alcohol. He's tipsy with delight over the corruption he's wrought on earth. But his doom is sure. He faces not only judgment, but also annihilation. He'll use whatever weapons he can to battle against you. I've found that he's very effective in using fear, worry, and anxiety to distract me from my focus on Christ. I battle back by praying, worshiping, and reading my Bible every day.

## PREPARE FOR BATTLE.

In his war on the saints, the devil seeks to keep us from trusting in God's love and pouring out our hearts in prayer. Prayer is the key to breaking strongholds and releasing God's power into the world.

Just think about praying for a sick person who is healed. Not discounting the God-given wisdom medical professionals bring to bear on sickness and injury, as we pray for the sick, we assault the strongholds of sickness or injury as God's agents of grace and power. Proactive intercession and declaration of God's Word release Kingdom power from the supernatural into the natural through us.

Now don't miss this: If no one had taken time to pray for Cathy, she may have given in to the enemy and committed suicide.

Prayer releases *dunamis*—recreative, liberating, supernatural power. You have much to do with what happens in the future. The Lord gave me this prophetic word while I was reflecting on this chapter:

*The future is fluid, moving, dependent on the prayers of the saints. My people can and do change the course of history when they commit to active intercession. The enemy of your souls is empowered by passivity in the ranks of the saints, and likewise he is often thwarted by the prayers of the faithful. Now understand this truth: the devil is already defeated. His life is ebbing away as we draw near to the end of the age. He has many strongholds, but none more deadly than human hearts; for those dark fortresses are lairs of evil that have an outlet in the natural.*

*You, and all other men and women of faith, have one great advantage over the devil. It is not just the fact that you know the devil exists; it is the crucial awareness of the power of my blood, shed for all humankind. My blood defeated him. Blood shed by the perfect Lamb sealed the devil's fate. Don't for a second think that he is defeated in the natural yet, but his time is running out. He is in his early death throes because he knows his time is short.*

## Take Charge of Your Destiny
### Principle Four:
### The devil doesn't have any power over you that you can't overcome with the authority of Christ.

# ACTION STEPS

### STEP ONE: USE YOUR SPIRITUAL AUTHORITY.

Every Christian has God-given spiritual authority. When you received Jesus as your Savior, the Holy Spirit took residence in your heart. The Spirit's wise counsel (see James 1:5); spiritual power and love (see Rom. 5:5); and authority (Matt. 28:18-20) are available to you in fulfilling your destiny. What you must realize is that the devil will do whatever he can to thwart your efforts in doing God's will and bringing His Kingdom to earth. Passivity leads to oppression and spiritual weakness. That's why you must exercise your spiritual authority if you want to fulfill your destiny and see God's Kingdom come to earth one heart at a time.

Words have creative *and* destructive power. Jesus spoke life into Lazarus' dead body (see John 11) and death to a fruitless fig tree (see Matt. 21:18-22). Your words also have power to bring life or death (see Prov. 18:21). That's why the devil tempts you to verbalize negatives rather than positives.

To combat the enemy's vicious assaults, you must command him to flee in Jesus' name (see James 4:7). Resisting him removes his spiritual footholds (see Eph. 4:27) and forces him to retreat.

Jesus says that the devil cannot overcome the Body of Christ, "...on this rock I will build my church, and the gates of Hades will not overcome it" (Matt. 16:18). God has equipped you with His power and authority to tear down strongholds (see 2 Cor. 10:4), take back what the enemy has stolen, and overcome anything the devil uses against you to keep God's Kingdom from advancing.

Many Christians are learning to apply God's Word in spiritual warfare prayer and proclamation just like Jesus did during His wilderness experience (see Matt. 4:1-11). They're claiming

God's promises and speaking them aloud into the spiritual atmosphere and retaking territories inhabited by evil. Your prayers also have incredible power to overcome evil.

Remember that the devil doesn't have any power over you that you can't overcome with the authority of Christ. Use your God-given authority and command the devil to leave your body, mind, emotions, children, marriage, home, neighborhood, church, and community alone—in Jesus' name. Expect God to move in the supernatural as you pray in the natural.

### Step Two: Give God Credit For Every Victory.

You must be very careful not to allow the enemy to gain a foothold in your ego. Pride is a Christian's downfall. I believe the main reason Christian leaders fall is that they slowly develop an "exception to the rules" mentality. You are God's son or daughter, but you're still accountable for your actions. In fact, "to whom much is given much is expected" (Luke 12:48).

Always give God the glory for the blessings you experience. Remember that "before his downfall a man's heart is proud, but humility comes before honor" (Prov. 18:12). Let God give you the honor He has chosen for you as you give Him the glory for all He does in and through you.

## Conclusion

You're armed and dangerous. You've been equipped to resist all of the enemy's flaming darts. Cultivate a pure heart and ask the Lord to empower you, and remember that the power at work in you has no limits. It emanates from God in Heaven and manifests in the miraculous on earth. Let Heaven invade your life and you'll see God transform your inner being, free you from fear, increase your faith, sharpen your understanding of His Word, and equip you to break through any obstacle the devil has placed in your path.

Use your God-given authority and power in accordance with His will, and you'll bring His Kingdom to earth. It's your destiny to represent God as Heaven's ambassador wherever you go. Let the Lord lead your life and you'll overcome the enemy's influences one battle at a time.

In the next chapter, I'll discuss God's mandate to live daily at a savoring pace by slowing down, resting in the Lord, and avoiding the temptation to be hasty.

### Endnotes

1. Jack Hayford, *Prayer Is Invading the Impossible* (Plainfield, NJ: Logos International, 1977), 64.

2. Myles Monroe, *Rediscovering the Kingdom: Ancient Hope for Our 21st Century World* (Shippensburg, PA: Destiny Image, 2004), 83.

# CHAPTER 5

# Don't Be Hasty

*It is not good to have zeal without knowledge, nor to be hasty and miss the way. —King Solomon* (Proverbs 19:2)

Haste is an attitude of the heart that reacts to situations with impatience and false confidence. —My Journal (February 26, 2007)

There's waste in haste.

During the recent gas crisis, my car was nearing empty when I spotted a service station advertising a three-cent savings. Excited to get a good deal, I zipped in looking for an open pump. I was eagerly backing into the only available slot when I heard a loud *crunch*. I'd brushed against the cement post guarding the attendant's booth. I couldn't believe it!

I left that station too embarrassed to get out and pump gas. My car was dented, my ego bruised, and our checking account was soon $700 lighter. I calculated I'd need to buy 23,000 gallons at a three-cent discount to make up the difference. I don't sweat gas prices anymore.

Haste takes many forms in people's lives. Working on Capitol Hill, I've seen a well-dressed executive spill hot coffee down his trousers while dashing to catch a closing elevator and a young intern break her spiked heel tripping on a curb while running for a bus.

The latest misstep I witnessed was a young lady wearing sandals running up an escalator. That's right, she was wearing flip-flops and running full speed uphill. You can imagine the mess she made of her shin when she fell against the metal stairs.

Hasty driving in Washington DC has proven costly for thousands. Red-light and speed cameras are netting the District millions. And recently, a hasty METRO bus driver killed two pedestrians in a crosswalk. He's facing vehicular manslaughter charges—all because he was more concerned about taking a quick right on red than paying attention to pedestrians. Trying to save a few seconds cost two precious lives.

Haste takes countless forms, many of which break hearts, ruin reputations, and waste hard-earned money.

## Adrenaline and Stress

Hasty lifestyles are in vogue, but at what cost? To name a few: adrenaline addiction, financial and relationship challenges, and personal embarrassment.

Adrenaline was my addiction of choice early in my naval career. I'm amazed at how easy it was for me to push myself to my limits. I'd often work 16 hours a day at sea.

In port, I'd zoom around my ship for ten hours visiting and counseling sailors, leading Bible studies and prayer meetings, and still have energy to tackle my five collateral duties.

But Saturdays in port were my crash days.

I was often bedridden with migraine headaches so severe I'd have to sleep for hours to recover. I had no idea I was an adrenaline junky. It took years to admit I was hurting myself with nonstop activity. I reasoned I was doing God's work, so it must have been His will for me to rush around like I did.

I lived at a frenetic pace every day. Yes, I was an adrenaline addict and didn't know it. At what pace are you living?

Dr. Archibald D. Hart warns us:

At the very core of the stress problem is the Western, twentieth-century lifestyle. The lives of most of us are too hectic and fast-paced. We are driven by a need to succeed, and our hectic lives leave little room for relaxation. It's as if we are trapped on a runaway train and don't know where the brakes are—or the engines of our bodies are jammed at full throttle. And Christians are not immune from the ravages of stress disease, because being a Christian doesn't necessarily mean being free of stress! Sometimes it may mean being under even greater stress, because trying to live a godly life in a godless world can take its toll.[1]

## COMBAT CHANGED MY LIFE.

It was in the Saudi Arabian desert that I discovered a life-transforming truth. One night following an enemy artillery bombardment, I was in my 4-foot-deep hole reading my Bible. For the first time I really understood what Paul was saying in Ephesians 1 about who we are and how we should live. Listen to his insightful words:

*In Him [Jesus] we were also chosen, having been predestined according to the plan of Him who works out everything in conformity with the purpose of His will, in order that we, who were the first to hope in Christ, **may be for the praise of His glory*** (Ephesians 1:11-12).

Did you get it? "Be," not "do"! We *exist* for God's glory. We don't exist to work ourselves to death; we live to be for the praise of His glory! What a revelation for a workaholic.

I finally realized that Christianity isn't primarily about doing things for God. It's about being God's son or daughter. It's about an intimate, personal relationship with Father God.

We're redeemed to enjoy being God's family members, not just to do things for Him. Hurray!

It was a radically liberating revelation. I'd been going 100 mph since puberty and finally realized in my 39th year that God was more concerned with who I am than what I do for Him. I was an A+ personality type who experienced an immediate internal shift once I discovered that I wasn't made to work 'til I drop.

I actually felt my inner motor slow down that night.

Since my epiphany in 1991, I've gradually become more focused on cultivating my relationship with Father God and not seeking approval I already have as a child of the Most High. I'm no longer rushing through life on an adrenaline high. I still have a long way to go, but I'm more convinced than ever that hasty living inhibits intimacy with God and those around us.

Can you relax without feeling guilty? Or are you still striving to win God's affirmation and acceptance?

If you're an adrenaline junky like I was, read Dr. Archibald Hart's book, *Adrenalin and Stress: The Exciting New Breakthrough That Helps You Overcome Stress Damage.* Perhaps his perceptive insights will free you from your bondage to speed and busyness.

## FINANCIAL AND RELATIONSHIP CHALLENGES

Haste also leads to poor financial and relationship decisions because impulsive spending can lead to unmanageable debt or bankruptcy.

Picture the harried young couple needing a new vehicle. They drive their high-mileage car into a dealership. An experienced salesperson smiles as she rises from her cluttered desk and walks outside. If first impressions really are made in a matter of seconds, the auto vender already knows she has a sale. It's now just a matter of working the sale to make a hefty commission.

An hour later the young couple is basking in new vehicle odors. Even though they signed for a 5-year, 7 percent loan, they're feeling giddy about the "good deal" they got on their shiny new "electric everything" van. About two weeks after their inaugural parking lot dent, their first of 60 hefty payments comes due. A week later they discover they're pregnant and neglected to budget for the costs of starting a family and moving to a two-bedroom apartment.

And what about the 40-something father of three whose mid-life crisis leads him into a hasty affair? He chooses divorce over repentance and takes his wife of two decades to court. Not only does he end up paying his lawyer over $10,000, but his soon to be ex-wife spends even more so she doesn't lose the roof over her head.

In the end, everyone loses—especially the brokenhearted kids—all because a temporarily insane husband-turned-gigolo makes a hasty decision to throw away his wife, reputation, and future. And the affair? The woman involved dumps the deserting dad after a year for another impulsive male.

*Haste often makes a mess of people's lives.*

Shortly after coming to faith in Jesus, I was sitting in a college marketing class listening to a professor tell us how to manipulate consumers into buying things they don't need. He discussed supermarket strategies related to impulse buying, the positioning of the highest profit items at eye level, how packaging excites children, and many other ways to increase profit at a hasty consumer's expense.

Banks and marketing geniuses have also found out how to exploit overzealous credit-card users. The average interest rate for standard bank credit cards topped 19 percent in March 2007, compared to 16.5 percent in 2003. Approximately half of all credit-card holders pay only their minimum monthly payments.[2] That means many Americans will never pay off their credit cards. Kiplinger warns that buying now and running up credit card debt may not be the best strategy.

> They start out sounding like a good deal: Credit cards allow you to buy now and pay later…But as bills come due and interest charges rear their ugly head, perhaps you've realized that you've gone a little wild with your plastic. After all, it's a bit too easy to rely on your credit cards as a sort of get-out-of-jail-free card, allowing you to push your bills to the very back of your mind. The average credit card balance of consumers ages 25 to 34 is more than $5,000.[3]

Instant gratification is a serious threat to our finances and relationships. In a fast-food world, it's not uncommon for newly married couples to rack up a mountain of debt on new homes and furnishings. This is a major change from a generation or two ago when my wife and I were newly married and saved up for what we needed to start a family.

I've counseled scores of young military couples who were tens of thousands of dollars in debt because they "needed" a house full of furniture, the latest electronic gadgets, and sleek new cars and trucks. One military member confessed to taking monthly cash advances on one credit card to pay the minimum payment on another one. He went bankrupt.

Hasty decisions cost far more than money. So don't buy what you can't afford and put your finances and relationships in jeopardy. Slow down your spending, live within your means, and be content with what you can actually afford.

If you ask God to help you, He'll reveal to you the secret of being content with what you have and protect you from the negative consequences of living beyond your means. Paul tells us he found the secret of being content in any situation.

> …I have learned to be content whatever the circumstances. I know what it is to be in need, and I know what it

*is to have plenty. I have learned the secret of being content in any and every situation, whether well fed or hungry, whether living in plenty or in want. I can do everything through Him who gives me strength* (Philippians 4:11-13).

## PERSONAL EMBARRASSMENT

Do you recall the news article about Chicago Bears fan who told his fellow drinkers in a local bar he'd change his name to Peyton Manning if the Colts beat the Bears in the Superbowl? I wonder how the fan felt the morning after the Colts won Superbowl XLI.

Hasty words often bring embarrassment. That's why Solomon says, "Do you see a man who speaks in haste? There is more hope for a fool than for him" (Prov. 29:20).

Can you think of a time when you spoke without thinking? What comes to mind? Were you embarrassed?

I remember in my early teens a heated argument on a school bus between two of my classmates. I jumped into the fray, spoke without thinking, and the next thing I knew I'd committed to a fist fight. I broke my right hand on my opponent's forehead and missed most of the summer baseball season. I was so dumb!

Hasty words can lead to unanticipated violence and loss of relationships. Just think about the couple whose argument escalates into profanity and accusation. Both feel they're right, so neither is willing to apologize. If unforgiveness persists, it can lead to a hasty breakup. They are too proud or embarrassed to confess guilt, so they let the relationship die.

*And all over a few hasty words.*

As I was reflecting on the pace of my life, I journaled the following prophetic reflections:

*Haste is proceeding in a direction you choose without seeking My guidance. If you act without thinking and praying, you will usually miss the mark. Think of a farmer who plants seeds without first preparing the soil. He gets the job done quickly, but his crop will fail. Or the fisherman who casts his line only to pull it out a minute later. He won't catch fish if he doesn't wait until a fish finds his bait. Haste is rushing headlong into the future without prayerful consideration of the consequence of your actions. Haste wastes wood for carpenters and seed for farmers. Haste compels you to get something done quickly rather than done well.*

## FINDING THE BALANCE

Robert Updegraff says, "To get all there is out of living, we must employ our time wisely, never being in too much of a hurry to stop and sip life, but never losing our senses of the enormous value of a minute."[4]

Balance is the key. If your two-year-old is five feet from falling into a swimming pool, sprinting to his rescue is critical. If you're always living at 100 mph, as I was, it could kill you early. So how do you optimize your time without wearing out your mind, buying things you don't need, maxing out your credit cards, hurting those you love, or needlessly embarrassing yourself? Here are a few suggestions that may help you slow down, find contentment in simple things, and live longer.

*Take Charge of Your Destiny
Principle Five:
Don't be hasty and you'll avoid many of the pitfalls
that negatively affect other people's lives.*

## ACTION STEPS

### STEP ONE: THINK AND PRAY BEFORE YOU SPEAK OR ACT.

Why is haste bad? Because it isn't a reasoned response to crisis. It isn't a prayerful reaction to a threat or opportunity. Haste robs you of divine illumination and guidance. It gives you instant gratification, but often leads to long-term loss. It takes prayerful consideration of your options to produce long-term gains. Spontaneous reactions are occasionally fruitful in the short term and usually costly in the long term.

Christian scholar and author William Arthur Ward[5] has wisdom to offer those who speak before thinking and act before praying:

- Before you speak, listen.

- Before you write, think.

- Before you spend, earn.

- Before you invest, investigate.

- Before you criticize, wait.

Dr. Kirk Jones asks, "How much of our decision making is hampered by fast thinking?" His insightful response sheds light on the downside of a hasty life.

We are so used to thinking quickly that we do not access the harm of speeded-up judgments. Rushed thinking usually severely restricts our ability to envision viable options. How many times have we made poor decisions because we did not take the time to sit and stare at a matter? Our haste did not allow time for us to see what can be seen only through patient consideration. Often the consequences of a poor decision can be discerned in advance, through patient pondering beforehand. Some mistakes are unavoidable; others are manufactured by hasty decision making.[6]

You need God's wisdom in making important decisions. So tap that goldmine in prayer and meditation on God's Word. Wisdom is so essential to fulfilling your destiny that the Bible says it's "much better to get wisdom than gold, to choose understanding rather than silver!" (Prov. 16:16). It's easy to ask for wisdom. James promises, "If any of you lacks wisdom, he should ask God, who gives generously to all without finding fault, and it will be given to him" (James 1:5).

What's *not* easy is waiting until God reveals His insights to you! So think and pray before you speak or act and you'll avoid many of the pitfalls other people experience.

## STEP TWO: LIVE AT A SAVORING PACE.

What does it mean to live at a savoring pace? Again Dr. Kirk Jones[7] has wisdom to share with you:

> To savor is to taste or smell with pleasure, to relish, to delight in, to enjoy. The word has its origination in the Latin *sapere,* which means both "taste" and "be wise." The connection between the physical and the psychological inherent in that root has never been more important. Savoring pace yields the richer, brighter life that opens to us once we slow down enough to notice it more. Savoring pace challenges our frenzied pattern of paying attention to more with a gentle, yet persistent, appeal to pay more attention.[8]

If you were competing in the Boston Marathon, you'd run at nearly a constant pace for over 26 miles. Run too quickly and you may collapse, too slowly and you may not cross the finish line before everyone else goes home. You have to pace yourself to finish.

Pacing contributes to a long, healthy, and meaningful life—especially in a high-speed culture like ours. We have enough things due yesterday to stress us out! Living on the run every day may make you a bit wealthier, but it won't make you happier.

You must intentionally slow down, look around, and enjoy living rather than letting the fast pace of life rob you of the life you work so hard to secure. Why don't you do an experiment: sit down in a garden, at the beach, or on a mountain, and look around for a while—no music, no computer, no cell phone. What do you see, hear, and feel? Strange sensations?

*That's life!*

### STEP THREE: WAIT FOR GOD'S BEST.

In late 1997, while stationed in Hawaii, I was getting close to 20 years of active military service. I'd just completed my doctoral degree and was feeling excited about retiring from the Navy and going into teaching or pastoral ministry. In a matter of weeks, I'd received three incredible job offers. But not wanting to preempt God's plan for my life, I asked the Lord for permission to submit my retirement request. I prayed many times a day over the course of six weeks and sensed no definite leading.

During that time, my head was telling me to retire while my heart was telling me to wait for God's reply. At the end of the six weeks, my wife and I were invited to a dinner party in honor of the Chief of Navy Chaplains, who was visiting Oahu for a few days. Before dessert, he asked me to take a quick walk around our host's garden. After a few minutes of small talk, the admiral asked me to remain on active duty, offered me any available job, and requested I call him when I made my decision.

I wrestled with God in prayer for three days and nights. Early on the fourth morning, the Lord spoke in my heart, *"If you get out, I'll bless your ministry; but if you stay, I'll bless you more.*" Based on that word from God, I stayed in the Navy even though I still wanted to retire in Hawaii.

God would have loved me no matter which option I chose, but His greater blessing—even though it meant staying on active duty—was retiring five years later and transitioning to the Senate Chaplain's Office where I now serve. Had I not prayed and waited before submitting my retirement request, I would not be on Capitol Hill experiencing God's greater blessing.

It's not always easy to wait for God's best—His best job, spouse, school, home—His best anything. But God's best is just that—His best. Perhaps you're impatiently waiting for a spouse, a job, or a new focus for your life. Whatever you are longing for may or may not be God's best.

Pray! Seek the Lord in worship. Let Him know your needs. Then ask God to help you wait until He answers your prayer. You must learn to wait for the Lord to move on your behalf if you hope to fulfill your destiny. His best for you always leads toward that end.

## CONCLUSION

You need to resist the pull of haste and stand firm in your faith in God's ability to bless you in His time. Hasty decisions, words, and actions will lead you into painful places. You face the risk of burnout, financial and relationship challenges, and personal embarrassment if you don't think and pray before you speak and act, live at a savoring pace, and wait for God's best.

Rest assured that in time, the Lord will fulfill what He promises in Psalm 84:11, "For the Lord God is a sun and shield; the Lord bestows favor and honor; no good thing does He withhold from those whose walk is blameless."

In the next chapter, I'll discuss how important it is to love God and others if you hope to experience a deeply meaningful life. God's love empowers you to live a life of love and bring His Kingdom to earth when you do His will.

## ENDNOTES

1. Archibald D. Hart, *Adrenalin and Stress: The Exciting New Breakthrough That Helps You Overcome Stress Damage* (Dallas: Word Publishing, 1991), 3–4.

2. http://www.hoffmanbrinker.com/credit-card-debt-statistics.html (May 2007).

3. http://www.kiplinger.com/features/archives/2007/02/ccmoves.html (May 2007).

4. Robert Updegraff in *Inspirational Quotes*.

5. William Arthur Ward (1921–1994), Christian American educator and author of over 100 articles, poems, and meditations.

6. Dr. Kirk Byron Jones, *Addicted to Hurry: Spiritual Strategies for Slowing Down* (Valley Forge: Judson Press, 2003), 10.

7. Dr. Jones is the author of several best-selling books including *Rest in the Storm: Self-Care Strategies for Clergy and Other Caregivers,* published by Judson Press.

8. http://www.savoringpace.com/history.html.

CHAPTER 6

# Care for Others

*But a Samaritan, as he traveled, came where the man was; and when he saw him, he took pity on him. He went to him and bandaged his wounds, pouring on oil and wine. Then he put the man on his own donkey, took him to an inn and took care of him. The next day he took out two silver coins and gave them to the innkeeper. "Look after him," he said, "and when I return, I will reimburse you for any extra expense you may have." —The Parable of the Good Samaritan (Luke 10:33-35)*

Love feels no burden, thinks nothing of trouble, attempts what is above its strength, pleads no excuse of impossibility; for it thinks all things lawful for itself, and all things possible. It is therefore able to undertake all things, and warrants them to take effect, where he who does not love, would faint and lie down. —Thomas à Kempis (Roman Catholic Monk, 1379–1471)

When we care for others, we're imitating Jesus—the ultimate lover of humankind.

The love of husband and wife reaches close to the love He feels for us. I remember sitting in my office on an exceptionally hot summer day in Virginia Beach when the phone rang. On the other end of the line was a senior Navy petty officer whose wife of six years was dying of ovarian cancer. For over a year I'd been providing pastoral care to the family.

"Chaplain," he said, "the doctor says 'Sheila' could die this afternoon. Would you come to the hospital?"

"Sure, I'm on the way...." I kept praying as I drove across town, parked, and walked to Sheila's room. *God, what do you want me to say?*

When I arrived, the 27-year-old mother of two beautiful sons was barely alive. Her husband, "Ben," was sitting on the bed holding her limp hand. I sat on the opposite side of the bed as the heart monitor began slowing down. We wept quietly as Sheila slipped away and realized her end was near. I suggested Ben say goodbye.

He leaned toward his wife's right ear and said, "I love you, darling." That's when a minor miracle occurred. Immediately, the heart monitor accelerated and color came back into Sheila's face. She slowly turned her head toward Ben and whispered, "I love you, too." And then she died. For a moment, we felt God's presence in the room. That's when I realized how powerful love really is. How powerfully a Christian man and woman can love one another even at the moment of death.

Five years later I was visiting the Norfolk Naval Base chapel when Ben came up to me with his two sons in tow. He asked me if I remembered him; I certainly did. He said that after Sheila died, God visited and comforted him, saying that she had run the race well and was now experiencing her reward for faithful service.

*Christians die well.*

Sheila certainly did. Other Christians I've been with at the point of death also died well. They were sold out for the Lord, and it showed in every aspect of their lives—including their deaths. They were imitators of God and dearly loved by God. They had no doubt where they were heading—Heaven.

Paul commends us to:

*"Be imitators of God, therefore, as dearly loved children and live a life of love, just as Christ loved us and gave Himself up for us as a fragrant offering and sacrifice to God"* (Ephesians 5:1-2).

Love is lived daily in caring for God, others, and ourselves. It's lived in sacrificial service. In living well and dying well. Jesus says:

*"Love the Lord your God with all your heart and with all your soul and with all your mind." This is the first and greatest commandment. And the second is like it: "Love your neighbor as yourself"* (Matthew 22:36-39).

Life is about love.

Without love for God, others, and yourself, your life will have no ultimate meaning.

## JESUS LIVED A LIFE OF LOVE.

Jesus was the ultimate lover—He loved everyone around Him. What did He know that we need to know? He realized that true love sees the best in others. The love He demonstrated was sacrificial love that validated the worth of others. It saw beyond sickness, despair, ethnicity, and gender. It saw others as Father God sees them. That's Heaven's love. It flowed from God's heart, through Jesus' heart, into the hearts of others and transformed their lives.

*It's agape.*

Jesus' love wasn't greedy or demanding, it was giving and liberating. Take, for example, His confrontation with Israel's religious leaders when they brought Him a woman caught in adultery. According to Jewish law (see Lev. 20:10) she should have been put to death. The encounter was actually a devious plot to accuse Jesus of disregarding the Law.

The scheme was foiled when love prevailed over loveless legalism. What does the following narrative tell you about Jesus' love for the adulterous woman? John records the confrontation.

> *"Teacher, this woman was caught in the act of adultery. In the Law Moses commanded us to stone such women. Now what do you say?" They were using this question as a trap, in order to have a basis for accusing Him. But Jesus bent down and started to write on the ground with His finger. When they kept on questioning Him, He straightened up and said to them, "If any one of you is without sin, let him be the first to throw a stone at her." Again He stooped down and wrote on the ground. At this, those who heard began to go away one at a time, the older ones first, until only Jesus was left, with the woman still standing there. Jesus straightened up and asked her, "Woman, where are they? Has no one condemned you?" "No one, sir," she said. "Then neither do I condemn you," Jesus declared. "Go now and leave your life of sin"* (John 8:4-11).

Jesus valued a woman considered worthless in a society where outward observance of laws had replaced loving God and neighbor. Jesus didn't excuse the woman's sin—He forgave her and admonished her in love to avoid future indiscretions. That's how God deals with anyone responding positively to His loving overtures. He forgives and forgets, removes guilt, and bestows grace. Then He commissions those He redeems to live a life of love.

## No Greater Love Exists.

At Father God's request, Jesus humbled Himself by setting aside His glory, taking human form, and living 33 years on earth. When His mission reached its pinnacle, He paid the ultimate price by taking the world's sins to a cross.

Paul tells us that Jesus:

*...being in very nature God, did not consider equality with God something to be grasped, but made Himself nothing, taking the very nature of a servant, being made in human likeness. And being found in appearance as a man, He humbled Himself and became obedient to death—even death on a cross!* (Philippians 2:6-8)

Jesus died for the complete forgiveness of your sins. His blood blotted out your transgressions. Not some of your sins— all of your sins: past, present, and future. Isn't that incredible?

Love motivated Him to die so you may live forever with Him in heaven. "Greater love has no one than this, that he lay down his life for his friends" (John 15:13). Jesus suffered the humiliation of rejection, denial, beating, whipping, kicking, spitting, mocking, nakedness, exhaustion, crucifixion, and thirst until He finally gave up His Spirit after six torturous hours on the cross. At any time He could have called for legions of angels to free Him. Instead, He chose the bitter road of humiliation and death so you could experience His unmerited gift of salvation.

*Agape* led Jesus to the cross.

*Agape* kept Jesus on the cross.

*Your Savior loves you that much.*

## JESUS CALLS EVERY CHRISTIAN TO LIVE A LIFE OF LOVE.

Not only did Jesus role-model sacrificial love and care for others, He tells His followers to live a life of love. "A new command I give you: Love one another. As I have loved you, so you must love one another" (John 13:34). What is agape (sacrificial love) in practical application? Paul tells us,

*Love is patient, love is kind. It does not envy, it does not boast, it is not proud. It is not rude, it is not self-seeking, it is not easily angered, it keeps no record of wrongs. Love does not delight in evil but rejoices with the truth. It*

*always protects, always trusts, always hopes, always per-severes* (1 Corinthians 13:4-7).

Do you love others like this? Not sure? Then substitute your first name for the word love in the passage above and read it aloud. Go ahead and do that right now.

Feeling troubled? Me too. I fall far short of Jesus' ideal application of *agape*. As I sit here at my computer, I remember being grumpy with my son on the phone last night and feeling so convicted that I called him back to apologize. I'm reminded of feelings, attitudes, and irritations that clearly demonstrate my shortfall. But I'm not giving up trying to live a life of love. Why?

Love is the most powerful force on the planet. It's the only hope for humankind.

As I reflected on the power of love and its potential for making the world a better place, I journaled these thoughts from the Lord:

*My child, why is it important that we love one another? It is important because love is what binds our hearts together in an unshakable commitment to preserving our relationship at all costs. I preserved our relationship by dying to make it possible and in continuing to pour out Myself into you to sustain its vibrancy. It is sacrificial love that maintains an intense passion between two hearts. Selfishness only thwarts attempts to come close. Sacrificial love fuels intimacy as we give to one another for the other's sake.*

*Humans have a tendency to pull back when things get tough. They let go of commitments too easily when things get hard. It's in the hardest times that love can grow most deeply. It is often on the verge of greater love that love is lost. What seems like an impossible challenge to love often turns out to be its greatest test and greatest victory. Love triumphs when it is allowed to suffer great loss without actually losing its vibrancy. The furnace of affliction, testing, and trial is where love is purified. It is only proven genuine when it is tested.*

*Love must be patient and kind. It must be resilient and flexible, for when it is brittle it looks strong until affliction comes, and then it shatters far too easily. Love proves genuine when it is put to the test. Will love forgive a wrong? Will it go the extra mile? Will it look for the good in others rather than the bad? Will it take upon itself the need to forgive when wronged? If so, that is love.*

*Love is My presence in you surging forth to change a selfish world one heart at a time. Listen to this. If love conquers all, then it takes the world back for Me. Love is the agent of change. Love is My presence transforming the world as it transforms heart after heart.*

*Love is like wind…it blows and you feel its effects, but you may not understand or see it except with the eyes of faith or a heart open to love.*

*Caring for others moves them into a place where true love is possible. It awakens a deep need within them as they experience true love. Love without demands opens a passageway in the human heart. It makes eternal connection possible because what you are doing when you give real love is spreading the fragrance of Heaven.*

That's the power of *agape*—love that positively changes the world one heart at a time.

## How Do We Care For Those Around Us?

A friend[1] of mine shared the following true story with me.

I was reminded [recently] of a story a colleague told me about the son of one of his closest friends from childhood. His friend's son, Jeremy, was a likable but odd boy, who always seemed to have his head in the clouds and was somewhat of a loner. His parents found it difficult to teach him responsibility, and he was forever losing things. He'd come home, having misplaced a new sweater or backpack. And they gave up on buying him lunchboxes because he could never keep track of one for more than a week. His parents, being good Dutch Protestants and living in a poor rural community, tried to discipline him so he would understand the value of his things, but nothing seemed to work. Once, he even came home having lost his sneakers. He just walked in barefoot and headed upstairs. When his mother asked him how in the world he could have lost his shoes, he just shrugged, said he was sorry, and that he'd try harder to keep track of his belongings in the future.

My colleague told me this story because tragically, Jeremy was killed in an auto accident earlier this year while a junior in high school, and my colleague attended the memorial service with the family. He said that when they showed up, they were stunned to see hundreds of students filling the pews. The pastor asked if anyone would like to say any words about Jeremy, and one after another, Jeremy's classmates came forward to talk about how kind and generous he was, of how he was always helping others. One boy told how his single mother couldn't afford to buy him shoes one year, and after complaining about how his feet hurt during PE, Jeremy pulled him aside, unlaced his sneakers, and gave them to him. A girl told how she came to school without a jacket one winter and how when Jeremy saw her shivering; he simply took the one off his back and gave it to her.

For almost 45 minutes, students came forward to tell their own story of this odd, quiet boy who gave all that he had. Needless to say, his parents were undone, and the students grew closer through their sharing. For Jeremy, at such a young age, had been acting as an anonymous agent of Christ, spreading the leavening of God's Kingdom throughout that community.

This heartrending tribute to a caring young man shows us the incredible power of love in action. Imagine how proud his grieving parents felt, hearing the amazing testimonies of their deceased son's charity. I wonder if Jeremy realized that he was living Paul's command to "do nothing out of selfish ambition or vain conceit, but in humility consider others better than your-selves" (Philippians 2:3). He gave without expectation of reward. He cared for those around him to the point of personal sacrifice.

*Jeremy lived agape and made the world a better place one heart at a time. Are you living an agape life?*

Whatever you do to make someone else's life better releases God's love and furthers His Kingdom. That's what you're here for—to make the world a better place. Be salt and light in a world desperately in need of knowing our loving God. How? Ask God for opportunities to care for those around you.

*Take Charge of Your Destiny*
*Principle Six:*
*Care for those around you.*

## ACTION STEPS

### STEP ONE: LISTEN AND SPEAK GRACIOUSLY.

Cultivate the gift of listening to others. Listeners are a rare breed in our busy culture—talkers are much more common. Follow James' advice and "be quick to listen, slow to speak and slow to become angry" (James 1:19). Ask open-ended questions and wait for complete responses. Don't interrupt to make your point; let others have their say. If you have children, make time to sit and chat with them rather than just correct them for messy rooms, spilled milk, or tardiness.

Be intentional when you speak, because you're responsible for your carelessly spoken words. Jesus says, "I tell you this, you must give an account on judgment day for every idle [or careless] word you speak" (Matt. 12:36, nlt). The Bible also says that "a word aptly spoken is like apples of gold in settings of silver" (Prov. 25:11) and "words from a wise man's mouth are gracious, but a fool is consumed by his own lips" (Eccles. 10:12). It's clear that careless, biting words will negatively impact those we love, while carefully chosen words will be a blessing to others.

### STEP TWO: SERVE OTHERS JOYFULLY

Serve others in love. Paul says:

*For you have been called to live in freedom, my brothers and sisters. But don't use your freedom to satisfy your sinful nature. Instead, use your freedom to serve one another in love* (Galatians 5:13 NLT).

Do the dishes when it's not your turn. Bring a meal to a sick neighbor. Open a door for someone. Cut a stranger's lawn. Volunteer your time. Be careful to keep your promises and commitments. Call your parents, siblings, and children at unexpected times of the week. Send uplifting e-cards, letters, text messages, or emails. Look for creative ways to bless others and God will bless you with deep joy. When people ask you why you're being so caring, tell them you love Jesus and you love them. God may open the door for you to lead them to Christ.

### STEP THREE: PRACTICE EXTRAVAGANT GIVING.

This is not just a pitch for tithing to your local church—though I think that's every Christian's duty. No, I'm talking about acts of care and concern that immediately impact those in need. Holidays are an exceptionally good time to look for ways to bless others. Have you ever seen the look on a cashier's face when you buy two gift cards and then give one back as a gift?

It's priceless.

People are really caught off guard when you bless them at unexpected times of the year. Think of ways to care for those in your immediate circle of friends and those you see often, like grocery clerks, hairstylists, wait staff, trash collectors. A gift card or even a box of homemade cookies with a big red bow could cheer up their whole week.

Jesus says, "Give, and it will be given to you. A good measure, pressed down, shaken together and running over, will be poured into your lap. For with the measure you use, it will be measured to you" (Luke 6:38). Not just a payback—a blessing—great joy in making someone else's life better, if only for a few moments. Look for someone in need—just one soul at a time—and bless that person.

Yes, look for the "one" in need as Heidi and Roland Baker do in Mozambique. Millions have been touched by their care, compassion, and love, one heart at a time.

In their July 2007 Iris Ministries newsletter, Heidi writes of the joy she feels in caring for those God has brought into her life:

Jesus has mercifully allowed me to not only sip from the cup of suffering, but also to drink fully from His cup of joy. After the challenges of feeding 50,000 people a day, the flood relief, bombings and monster cyclones, Jesus has brought me joy unspeakable and full of glory this June. This month I loved cheering King Jesus on as He brilliantly shined His liquid glory love into the darkness of the unreached Makua tribe. Seeing village after village run to King Jesus makes me fall even more in love with Him. I love my life, and I love Him more than life! What a privilege to be alive when the harvest is so ripe and the Lord of the harvest is sending forth laborers (see Matt. 9:36-40). We must lift up our eyes to see that the harvest is indeed ripe and ready (John 4).

## CONCLUSION

Give as you are able. Care for others. Live a life of love and make the world a better place. That's every Christian's mandate. You were born again when you accepted Christ as your Savior and His Spirit took up residence in your heart. God literally poured agape into your heart when He empowered you to live a holy life (see Rom. 5:5). So trust in the Lord with all your heart and then make the world a better place by loving and caring for those around you.

In the next chapter, you'll learn what it means to partner with God in bringing His Kingdom to earth. You were created and empowered to make a significant difference in the lives of those around you. To do so, you must tap the wellspring of God's superabundant presence and allow Him to direct the course of your life.

### ENDNOTE

1. I'm indebted to Eric Sapp for sharing with me his July 8, 2007, sermon on *The Kingdom of God,* in which he included this illustration.

# CHAPTER 7

# Partner With God

*When Jesus had called the Twelve together, He gave them power and authority to drive out all demons and to cure diseases, and He sent them out to preach the Kingdom of God and to heal the sick....So they set out and went from village to village, preaching the gospel and healing people everywhere. —Doctor Luke (Luke 9:1-2, 6).*

The normal Christian life is a partnership between God and each of us, played out in everyday living as we become the gate of heaven, releasing the manifestation of God's reality for those around us. Paul called us co-laborers with Christ [see 2 Corinthians 6:1] and that is what we are—partners in the work of Heaven in this earthly sphere....We are co-laborers, meaning that apart from Christ our work is not complete, and at the same time, amazingly, *His work on Earth is not complete without us.* God looks to you and me as contributors to what He is doing, not just as robots carrying out His ideas. He's actually interested in your desires and dreams and has opened up His plan on this planet to your influence.[1] —Bill Johnsons

You were created with a specific purpose in mind.

The purpose of your life has much more to do with God than it does with you. As Rick Warren says:

The purpose of your life is far greater than your own personal fulfillment, your peace of mind, or even your happiness. It's far greater than your family, your career, or even your wildest dreams and ambitions. If you want to know why you were placed on this planet, you must begin with God. You were born *by* his purpose and *for* his purpose.[2]

*God needs your help.*

He needs you to take charge of your destiny and fulfill your purpose—bringing His Kingdom to earth by doing His will. That's exactly what Jesus commissioned His disciples to do and that's also what He's calling you to do. Jack Hayford says:

> Almost everyone knows that the Lord Jesus Christ promised to return again. But too few of us realize that in the interim we are not merely charged to witness of His love while waiting for His return. We also are explicitly commanded to introduce His rulership—the Kingdom of God—into those circumstances in which man's lost rule has produced impossible situations.[3]

God calls every Christian to partner with Him in doing His will and dethroning the powers of darkness. The more of us who commit to partnering with God, the faster His Kingdom will spread around the world. David Chilton tells us:

> The Kingdom was established when Christ came. But it has not reached its full development. Like a mustard tree, it started out small, but will grow to enormous size...The Kingdom will grow in size, spreading everywhere, until the knowledge of God covers the earth, as the waters cover the sea. The Kingdom's growth will be *extensive*.

But the Kingdom will also grow *intensively*. Like leaven in bread, it will transform the world, as surely as it transforms individual lives. Christ has planted into the world His Gospel, the power of God unto salvation. Like yeast, the power of the Kingdom will continue to work "until *all* is leavened."[4]

Right now millions of Christians are partnering with God and bringing His Kingdom to Earth. All around the world, those walking in God's delegated power and authority are taking back what legally belongs to the Body of Christ. They're sharing the Gospel of the Kingdom, leading the lost to salvation, making disciples, healing the sick, and delivering the oppressed. They're bringing the Kingdom message to the marketplace, government, entertainment, college campuses, military, professional sports, media, and churches, at home and abroad. The Kingdom is spreading—no power on earth can stop it.

Will you partner with God by spreading the Gospel of His Kingdom just like our Lord Jesus and His disciples did?

## THE GOSPEL OF THE KINGDOM WAS THE EARLY CHURCH'S MESSAGE AND MISSION.

After His resurrection, Jesus commissioned His followers to go into the world and make disciples, not just converts:

> *All authority in heaven and on earth has been given to Me. Therefore go and **make disciples of all nations,** baptizing them in the name of the Father and of the Son and of the Holy Spirit, and teaching them to obey everything I have commanded you. And surely I am with you always, to the very end of the age* (Matthew 28:18-20).

Then Jesus kept appearing and teaching them about the Kingdom.

*He presented Himself alive after His suffering by many*
*proofs, appearing to them during forty days and speak-*
*ing about the kingdom of God"*(Acts 1:3 ESV).

Prior to His ascension into Heaven, Jesus said to the disciples, "Do not leave Jerusalem, but wait for the gift my Father
promised, which you have heard me speak about. For John baptized with water, but in a few days you will be baptized with the
Holy Spirit" (Acts 1:4-5). His promise was fulfilled ten days
later on the Jewish festival of Pentecost when the Holy Spirit
came upon 120 disciples gathered in an upper room.

*When the day of Pentecost came, they were all together in*
*one place. Suddenly a sound like the blowing of a violent*
*wind came from heaven and filled the whole house where*
*they were sitting. They saw what seemed to be tongues of*
*fire that separated and came to rest on each of them. All of*
*them were filled with the Holy Spirit and began to speak in*
*other tongues as the Spirit enabled them* (Acts 2:1-4).

In partnering with God, the disciples preached the good
news of the Kingdom of God, healed the sick, and cast out
demons just like Jesus did. Jesus was with the disciples (as He is
with us today) in the presence of His Holy Spirit empowering
their preaching and bringing healing and deliverance to the sick
and oppressed.

After the outpouring of the Holy Spirit at Pentecost, thousands were converted in a matter of days. Why? Signs and wonders accompanied the preaching of the Gospel and many gave
their hearts to the Lord. The sick and oppressed were liberated
physically and spiritually.

Beginning with Apostle James' martyrdom (see Acts
7:54-60) the church in Jerusalem came under intense persecution. Apostle Peter was eventually arrested by King Herod.
Because he was taken into custody during the Feast of

Unleavened Bread, the king decided to throw Peter in jail. In response, the church in Jerusalem battled in prayer for Peter's life. Luke tells us:

> *...Peter was kept in prison, but the church was earnestly praying to God for him* (Acts 12:5).

The night before Herod was to bring Peter to trial, an angel of the Lord released him from prison. His escape from captivity astounded the church and infuriated Herod. The church partnered with God by doing what they could do on Peter's behalf—they prayed earnestly. In response, God sent an angel to set Peter free (see Acts 12:6-16).

Apostle Paul also partnered with God in ministry and saw many give their hearts to Christ. God did many miracles through him. Listen to what Luke writes about Paul's ministry in Ephesus:

> *Paul entered the synagogue and spoke boldly there for three months, arguing persuasively about the kingdom of God. But some of them became obstinate; they refused to believe and publicly maligned the Way. So Paul left them. He took the disciples with him and had discussions daily in the lecture hall of Tyrannus. This went on for two years, so that all the Jews and Greeks who lived in the province of Asia heard the word of the Lord. **God did extraordinary miracles through Paul, so that even handkerchiefs and aprons that had touched him were taken to the sick, and their illnesses were cured and the evil spirits left them**￼* (Acts 19:8-12).

## PARTNER WITH GOD IN DOING KINGDOM BUSINESS.

Every follower of Christ is called to partner with God in proclaiming the Gospel of the Kingdom. History records the continuation of evangelism and miracles throughout the Christian era. During my doctoral program, I studied the works of the Holy Spirit in the life of the Church. Though some scholars have attempted to convince us that healing and deliverance miracles ended with the apostolic age, history is replete with accounts of healing and deliverance miracles.

I've witnessed God do many miracles. In upstate New York three decades ago, I severely injured my left ankle playing soccer at a youth retreat. I was "chosen" by the teens to be a goalie even though I'd never played soccer in my life. In a matter of minutes I was injured and limping painfully off the wet field. A day later, I was resting on our couch when a friend from home arrived for a brief visit. We decided to pray together. I asked for prayer for my painfully sprained, black and blue ankle. As our friend was praying for me I saw a flash of light go across my inner eyes toward my left ankle.

*I was healed immediately—no more pain, swelling, or black and blue remained.*

You can imagine my excitement. I'd never experienced a miracle before. After our friend left, I put on my exercise gear and went for a run, a miracle celebration 5K. I was overwhelmed by the reality of God's loving presence and power.

*God still does miracles.*

What an amazing revelation.

God opened my eyes to the miraculous—something I'd never heard about in my Baptist seminary. My ankle was healed and my heart yielded to God—I read the whole New Testament in a few weeks with increasing faith in God's willingness to heal the sick and deliver the oppressed.

I discovered the Gospel of the Kingdom was more than preaching salvation—as important as that is. Salvation leads sinners to Christ. The Kingdom Gospel leads sinners to Christ and empowers them with the Holy Spirit to partner with God in bringing His Kingdom to earth and overcoming the power of the enemy by healing the sick and setting free the demonically oppressed.

*That's really good news!*

What I'm talking about is the *normal Christian life* that many of the believers we know experience every day. It's the life the majority of our Christian brothers and sisters in Africa, South America, Asia, and in many other places where Christians are living right now.

They're passionately in love with Jesus and flow daily in His anointing. It's no accident that the church is growing so rapidly in non-Western countries.

But don't be discouraged. God hasn't abandoned the Western church. If you're open to God's power and love, He'll partner with you by working miracles as you proclaim His Kingdom and glory. If you're a leader and God is challenging you to partner with Him, ask the Holy Spirit to fill you with His power; then daily make yourself available to God. He'll gladly show you His plans and provide whatever you need to do His will.

As I was journaling about partnering with God in proclaiming the Gospel of the Kingdom, He asked me:

*What is the main focus of the Christian life, the life of Christ in you? It is following My leading in establishing My Kingdom. That is easier and more important than you realize. It is easier and more important because it is established in direct obedience to My guidance—not in you recreating programs and initiatives others found effective.*

*My plans are tailor-made, precise, specific. Seek My face and ask Me to show you what I want you to do. I have plans for individuals, families, and ministries. Partner with Me and I will anoint you to follow My plans so you will fulfill your destiny. I am able to do far more than you can imagine. I will raise you up for mighty works of grace if you*

*will just surrender your life to My purposes. Are you will-*
*ing to follow Me?*

*Take Charge of Your Destiny*
*Principle Seven:*
*You never run the race alone;*
*God is with you all the way.*

## ACTION STEPS

### STEP ONE: PARTNER WITH GOD IN PRAYER.

God chooses to limit His earthly activities by delegating Kingdom business to people just like you and me. He must have quite a sense of humor, an uncanny ability to pick the least qualified partners to assist Him in bringing His Kingdom to earth. That said, He's asking us to partner with Him in prayer.

God calls all Christians to pray. So what's the purpose of prayer? Untold volumes have been written on the subject, yet the object of prayer has never been simpler to understand. God is calling you to partner with Him by praying that His will may be done on earth as it is in Heaven, every day, in every place, by everyone. Isn't that an amazing challenge?

Prayer has too many historic forms and nuances to detail, yet prayer is most simply—talking to God as His Spirit brings His thoughts into your mind.

Here's an example:

Good morning Father. I praise You for the beauty and majesty of creation, for the spontaneous laughter of playing children, and the heartfelt love exhibited in a caring parent's watchful eyes. I give You praise for the great gift of salvation won for us by Jesus' death on the cross and the ever-present sense of love and acceptance You've poured into my heart.

Let me partner with You today and every day. I place myself at Your beck and call as You lead me to live for the praise of Your glory, and joyfully do Your will so Your Kingdom will be established in the hearts of those around me.

May You receive all the glory as Your Kingdom comes where Your will is done through my life. I'm available no matter what You require of me, so please interrupt the course of my day whenever You have a task to assign me. Make Your will so clear I can't possibly miss it and I will do my best to honor Your Name.

I love You, Lord, and pray for those in harm's way, the oppressed, the unsaved, the sick, and those on life's margins. Move in and through me as I lift up those who need Your help today...etc. In Jesus' Mighty Name, Amen."

### STEP TWO: PARTNER WITH GOD IN WORSHIP.

Worship releases God's power into the spiritual atmosphere around you. It empowers angelic hosts to do God's bidding and thwarts the enemy's attacks. When you feel tension in your heart or home—worship. When you feel the enemy attacking your mind, body, or emotions—worship. Worship has power to break through the gates of hell and reclaim lost territory for God. It liberates us from contrary emotions and empowers us for Kingdom service.

You may attend church once or twice a week, but you are the church 24/7. Worship is a victorious Christian's lifestyle. It's taking time to love God with your praises, thanksgiving, and heartfelt appreciation for His goodness and mercy. It's as simple as saying, "Yay, God," when you see Him working around you, or taking an hour to "soak" in His presence while listening to worship music.

During a recent five-day personal retreat, my wife and I arrived with heavy burdens for our congregation. On the third evening I was moved to lie face down on the floor and stretch out my hands as if to touch the foot of Jesus' cross.

As I worshiped, I was moved to tears in appreciation for the sacrifice Jesus made on my behalf—I cried for over a half hour and felt a weight on me so great I couldn't move. Eventually the weight lifted and God's joy filled me—I began to chuckle, then to laugh so hard I started to ache. For more than twenty minutes I was on the floor basking in the deepest joy I've felt in years, bliss so real that the Spirit enveloped me. It all began with worship. God met me in my need for renewal, accepted my worship, and blessed me with a love gift of His joy-giving presence.

Making worship an intentional part of your life aligns you in partnership with God and releases His power through your praises. If your church isn't very celebrative, worship at home with your family. Shout to the Lord, dance before Him, lift your hands, sing loudly—even if you don't sing well—when you're alone in the shower lift your praises to Him! Make joyful noise for God! He'll love it!

Why? Worshipers bless God!

At red lights, don't dwell on wasted seconds—use the opportunity to worship! During your commute to work, play worship CDs and learn the words as you sing joyfully to the Father. When you're exercising, play worship music—it'll build your spiritual stamina!

### Step Three: Partner with God in Kingdom Service.

I've heard that only one in ten Christians ever witness to a nonbeliever. Whether this is accurate or not, all Christians are called to an evangelical lifestyle. So why don't most Christians share their faith with others? Either they don't have anything substantial to share, are afraid of rejection, or are willing to witness for Christ but don't know how to share the Gospel of the Kingdom.

Why don't some Christians have a testimony to share? They may know about the Lord, but not know Him personally. It's hard to talk about someone you don't really know. The sad reality is that some people who dutifully attend church may not know Jesus as their personal Savior.

Here's the bottom line: Everyone in the Kingdom (born-again believers) is in the Church, but not everyone who goes to church is in the Kingdom. Going to church doesn't guarantee you're going to Heaven when you die. It's up to you to take responsibility for your future and make sure you've accepted Jesus as your Savior. The consequences of *not* doing so are very sad.

If you're a born-again Christian and can't muster the courage to share your faith with others for fear of offending them or being cast as "intolerant," then ask God to bring you opportunities to share Christ with others. God needs your help, remember? The best way to do this is praying every morning, "God, I'm available. Please bring someone to me so I may share Jesus with him or her." I often find the starting point in witnessing is asking people what their 100-year plan is. That often gets a conversation going.

*You'll get over the fear of rejection with God's help.*

God didn't give you a spirit of fear (see 2 Tim. 1:7), so if you have one, it's from the enemy. Ask God to give you courage and opportunities to witness. He will.

If you don't know how to witness to someone in detail, you *can* testify about what positive things Jesus has done in your life and bring them to your church. To learn more about the nuts and bolts of witnessing, read Paul Little's book, *How to Give Your Faith Away.*

Finally, on average, it takes ten contacts with Christians for someone to give his or her life to Jesus, so consider that God may have you planting a lot of seeds (as I most often do). Sometimes you'll get to pray with someone to accept Jesus as their Savior. Without discipleship, new converts often fall away from God, so invite them to church and introduce them to your pastor or cell group leader.

## CONCLUSION

God needs your help. As incomprehensible as that may seem, it's true! He's limited Himself to bringing His Kingdom to earth through partnering with the Body of Christ. We're the heralds of God's Kingdom. As frail, spiritually out of tune, and distracted by the world as you may sometimes be, the God of the universe has chosen you to bring His Kingdom to earth. It's a huge task, yet it requires just one act of obedience at a time. Are you ready to join God in this great work?

In the next chapter you'll learn that God promises to provide whatever you need to do His will and how walking in faithful obedience is what releases His provision from Heaven. Your first steps of faith are often the key to unlocking Heaven's storehouse on your behalf.

### ENDNOTES

1. Bill Johnson, *The Supernatural Power of A Transformed Mind: Access to a Life of Miracles* (Shippensburg: Destiny Image Publishers, Inc., 2005), 139–40.

2. Rick Warren, *The Purpose Driven Life* (Grand Rapids: Zondervan, 2002), 17.

3. Jack Hayford, *Prayer is Invading the Impossible* (Gainesville: Bridge-Logos Publishers, 1977), 19.

4. David Chilton, *Paradise Restored: A Biblical Theology of Dominion* (Horn Lake: Dominion Press, 2007), 74–75.

# CHAPTER 8

# Expect God's Provision

*The Lord is my shepherd, I shall not be in want.* —*King David* (Psalm 23:1)

"I believe in God the Father Almighty, Maker of Heaven and earth." What does this mean? I believe that God has made me and all creatures; that he has given and still preserves to me my body and soul, eyes, ears, and all my members, my reason and all my senses; also clothing and shoes, meat and drink, house and home, wife and child, land, cattle and all my goods; that he richly and daily provides me with all that I need for this body and life, protects me against all danger and guards and keeps me from all evil. —Martin Luther (1483–1546)

## GOD IS A GENEROUS PROVIDER.

A high school senior approached me after church and told me he was going to Bible college to prepare for the ministry. I was thrilled to hear such an enthusiastic announcement from an 18-year-old. I asked him what schools he'd applied to, and he just stared at me for a moment before saying,

"Well…none."

I asked him why he hadn't applied since it was only three months until graduation. He said he didn't have money for college. That's when I practiced active listening to make sure I understood him.

"So, are you saying that God is calling you into the ministry and you're not applying to colleges because you don't have any money?"

"Well, yeah."

"Okay," I said. "Let me see if I can clarify for you how to walk in God's will. If God is calling you into the ministry, then He's obligated Himself to provide everything you need to do His will. In faith, you must apply to colleges and ask God to provide whatever you need to fulfill His plan for your life. Then He'll either meet your financial needs miraculously or lead you to apply for scholarships, loans, or a part-time job. God will most likely provide the money as you need it and not all of it in advance so your faith will grow as you prepare for the ministry—do you get it?" He got it! That fall he began preparing for the ministry.

*Don't ever doubt that God loves you. You are family, a King's kid, an adopted co-heir of Christ!*

Provision is God's promise for every Christian. Paul says, "*...God will meet all your needs according to His glorious riches in Christ Jesus*" (Phil. 4:19). God has provided His only Son to be your Savior so you can trust Him to provide lesser gifts in equipping you to do His will.

Though your earthly father may not have been the best provider, your heavenly Father will provide everything you need for life and godliness (see 2 Peter 1:3). God's provision in Christ includes His unfailing love, forgiveness, healing, and guidance to fulfill your destiny. Your part is unconditional, joyful obedience to God's will as the Holy Spirit reveals it to you step by step. His plan is for spiritually minded Christians to bring His Kingdom to earth.

## WHAT DOES GOD REALLY WANT FROM YOU?

What's the main reason God has called you into His Kingdom? Many people think it's to do things that please God. That's true to a point, but the deeper reality is that He desires for you to come into His presence daily and enjoy His companionship. He wants a personal relationship with you! Really. He deeply desires an intimate two-way relationship with you.

*Seem too good to be true?*

Well, millions of Christians have taken the challenge of going deeper into the river of God's love. It's not painless—it's even a bit frightening at first because God is after all, *God*! He's a consuming fire as well as a loving Father.

But fear not! God loves you and His "perfect love drives out fear" (see 1 John 4:18).

What does God really want?

He wants you! He loves you and has provided all you need to enjoy an abundantly personal and meaningful relationship with Him. He's ready to bring you into his heart, so what's stopping you from giving yourself unreservedly to Him?

## THERE'S NO REASON TO HOLD BACK.

When you heard the Gospel, admitted you were a sinner in need of forgiveness, confessed your sins, and asked Jesus to be your Savior—you became a new creation. He totally forgave you. Then He initiated the sometimes painful, lifelong process of transforming you from the inside out. Sanctification is God's way of scrubbing out the residue (or stain) of sin from your old life. Your sins were forgiven when you accepted Jesus as your Savior, but your sinful thought patterns, compulsions, and negative attitudes are removed over time.

Even though you still sin occasionally, you're no longer under sin's condemnation. Jesus took that away when He died for you. Paul says,

*Therefore, **there is now no condemnation for those who are in Christ Jesus,** because through Christ Jesus the law of the Spirit of life set me free from the law of sin and death. For what the law was powerless to do in that it was weakened by the sinful nature, God did by sending His own Son in the likeness of sinful man to be a sin offering. And so He condemned sin in sinful man* (Romans 8:1-3).

*Now that's Good News!*

You're a new creation and God's ready to make you a spiritual warrior and a world changer. How? He'll lovingly challenge your values and ask you to alter your lifestyle. That's critical because a worldly (average American) lifestyle inhibits Kingdom service. Jesus says,

*If anyone would come after Me, **he must deny himself and take up his cross** and follow Me. For whoever wants to save his life will lose it, but **whoever loses his life for Me and for the gospel will save it.** What good is it for a man to gain the whole world, yet forfeit his soul? Or what can a man give in exchange for his soul?* (Mark 8:34-37).

As more of us take up our crosses daily and follow Jesus, the faster His Kingdom will spread to the ends of the earth. Then He will return. Listen to what Paul says:

*For as in Adam all die, so in Christ all will be made alive. But each in his own turn: Christ, the firstfruits; then, when He comes, those who belong to Him. **Then the end will come, when He hands over the kingdom to God the Father after He has destroyed all dominion, authority and power.** For He must reign until He has put all His enemies under His feet"* (1 Corinthians 15:22-25).

The Lord has chosen you to bring His Kingdom to earth as you do His will. That's your destiny. It takes sacrifice and spiritual maturity to follow the Holy Spirit's leading in doing God's will one act of obedience at a time. The cumulative effect of every Christian doing God's will dethrones the principalities of darkness and brings lost souls into God's wonderful light. The way up is actually down. The greatest in the Kingdom is the servant of all. I'm sad to say that some Christians aren't ready and willing to surrender their lives to Kingdom service. Why?

## GOD'S CURE FOR A SLUGGISH CHURCH

Many Christians are worldly—comfortable in an unfulfilling way, almost bored with life.

That's why so many live like the world; they haven't tapped into God's power and love. Carnal pleasures are inferior substitutes for God's loving presence.

Too many churchgoers rarely study the Bible, pray only in emergencies, and get edgy if their pastor preaches more than a 20-minute sermon. But they're really excited about jumping in the car after church and sprinting home to catch their favorite team on the tube.

*That makes God sad. Why?*

Because He has so much more for us. He's willing to provide anything and everything we need to do His will, but many Christians aren't interested in doing His will. They've been trained in spectator churches to do their own will in a never-ending pursuit of happiness. Satan must be thrilled to see how religious we've become. Why? He's not threatened by religious people—it's Kingdom-focused, Spirit-filled prayer warriors that scare him to death.

## KINGDOM SERVICE ISN'T FOR TIMID SOULS.

During his lifetime George Mueller cared for over 10,000 orphans, often 3,000 or 4,000 at a time, never asking for a single donation to feed, clothe, house, or educate his charges.

On one particularly lean day, the director of the orphanage begged Mr. Mueller to ask for donations because the cupboards were bare and there were hundreds of kids to feed. Mueller smiled and said, "God will provide." Feeling defeated, the director slumped into a rickety chair. As the boys streamed into the room and sat at empty tables, Mueller quieted them down and prayed, "I thank you, Lord that you will provide breakfast for the boys. I pray in Jesus' name, amen."

Within seconds there was a loud knock on the door. When the visitor was ushered into the dining room, he and his helpers were carrying baskets of sweet rolls—enough to feed all the boys. The baker said, "Mr. Mueller, last night I was awoken, and impressed by the Lord to bake for the boys. So I woke my assistants and here we are."

Just as the bakers were leaving, a horse-drawn cart broke down right in front of the orphanage. The driver was about to dump the large containers he was hauling until he realized where he was. He went to the orphanage door and knocked. "Mr. Mueller, Sir, my wagon wheel is broken so I need to dump my load in the gutter unless you have need of some fresh milk." And once again, one of Mr. Mueller's over 10,000 prayers had been answered by the Lord.

God called George Mueller to care for thousands of British orphans and provided the bounty needed to sustain them in many unexpected and miraculous ways. His life wasn't easy. Actually, it was very hard at times.

Kingdom life is sometimes messy around the edges. It means you may have to drive an inebriated stranger home in your car or gently ask a scantily clad walk-in counselee if she'd mind wearing your secretary's shawl during your session. It requires that you deal with those who may offend (or frighten) you with their attitudes, odor, language, or appearance. Fringe people—loved unconditionally by God, just like you.

The people Jesus hung out with were fringe people too: outcastes, ex-prostitutes, tax collectors, tough guys, Gentiles, cripples—people some church leaders wouldn't seat in the front row visitor's section or invite to lunch.

During our years in Hawaii, my family and I attended First Assembly of God at Red Hill. It's a church of many thousands. The first time we attended a Sunday evening baptism service, we were amazed to hear many new converts testify about their seedy lives prior to meeting Jesus.

Our senior pastor didn't mind messy. He and scores of outreach teams befriended anyone and everyone God brought to them. Many of them started attending one of the scores of discipleship courses offered weekly. Some even went to the foreign mission field after completing a year of training fully funded by the church.

Our pastor opened our eyes to those on life's margins where everyone matters to God and should also matter to us.

## PREPARE FOR PRUNING.

So what's God up to? Pruning. God's weeding out unproductive leaders and replacing them with humble, Kingdom-focused men and women. He's preparing the Church for battle.

Keep your eyes on the headlines—God's not finished removing indulgent, self-focused leaders—not just ministers, but politicians, sports figures, industry leaders, educators, entertainers, and many others. If you claim to be a Christian and you're living outside God's will, you're on dangerous ground. He will let you reap what you sow. Jesus says:

*I am the vine; you are the branches. If a man remains in Me and I in him, he will bear much fruit; apart from Me you can do nothing. **If anyone does not remain in Me, he is like a branch that is thrown away and withers; such***

*branches are picked up, thrown into the fire and burned*
(John 15:5-6).

God's calling His Church and its leaders to repentance and challenging us to "get beyond" our fears of associating with the seedy side of society. Christianity is a radical relationship with a radical Savior. We're called to walk in His steps. So get ready for radical ministry opportunities. The harvest to come will not be tidy—it will be challenging and rewarding, but not tidy.

The Lord challenged me to take a good look at my own heart. Here are some reflections from that early morning conversation:

*My children are dying on the streets, and you are not reaching out to them. You are letting your self-conceived ideas skew your vision of My Kingdom. A time of shaking is coming on the Church. I will pour out My Spirit on those whose hearts are surrendered to Me, but will you reject Me if your world is turned upside-down? Open your heart to My promises. I will provide what you need to do My will, but are you willing to do whatever I ask of you? Will you place your Isaac on my altar? Will you obey Me and move to far places if I command that of you? Will you open the doors of your heart, home, and church to the unchurched?*

*I am calling My church to repentance. Yes, I am tired of passive faith and sinful lives. I am calling you to action— radical action—by summoning from your midst those who will take My Word, My love, My forgiveness, and spread them like seeds on a fertile field.*

*A harvest is coming, but those unprepared for this work will be passed by like the virgins whose lamps had little oil. I am coming to ignite the fire of revival. Are you willing to accept those into your midst whose hearts I have broken?*

*Prepare, prepare for hungry masses to come to you seeking answers to life's deepest questions...*

As you can see, the Lord is saying that tough times are ahead—all because He desires to bring His Kingdom to Earth and too many hearts are closed to Him. The impact of 9/11 didn't move many to repentance. What *will* bring the masses to God if tragedies of that scale have little effect on the spirituality of a nation like ours? I shudder to consider what it will take to bring world-wide revival before Jesus returns.

If you commit yourself to Kingdom service and a holy life, you'll see God's substantive provision flow day by day. So, if you're willing to do what God is calling you to do, take a leap of faith, pray for specific guidance, get out of your comfort zone, and when you're given marching orders, enjoy an amazing journey. And don't worry, you can...

*Expect God's provision.*

He will provide what you need to do His will—HIS will, not yours. He's the Lord of the universe and He's waiting to see His Kingdom come where His will is done. You have an important role to play—God needs your help! He will provide all you need as you need it.

As Louis Cassels tells us:

If God wants you to do something, He'll make it possible for you to do it, but the grace he provides comes only with the task and cannot be stockpiled beforehand. We are dependent on him from hour to hour, and the greater our awareness of this fact, the less likely we are to faint or fail in a crisis.[1]

*Take Charge of Your Destiny*
*Principle Eight:*
*God will provide what you need to do His will.*

## ACTION STEPS

### STEP ONE: SEEK GOD'S WILL.

If you're ready to obey, God will make His will clear to you. So the first thing you need to do is determine *if* you are willing to do whatever God asks you to do. Once you settle that issue, the rest is straightforward.

Let me give you an example. I recently spoke at a pastors' retreat for 30 Christian leaders. During a break, my wife and I were strolling around a small pond when we came upon two pastors in deep conversation. One was a Farsi-speaking Baptist minister who asked us to pray about a decision he had to make. He'd been asked by three different groups to pastor Farsi-speaking congregations—one in California, another in Washington DC, and the other in Germany. He was in a quandary and quite worried that he might miss God's will.

I told him it wasn't his problem to figure out which call, if any, to take. He was amazed. When I told him he just needed to pray for guidance and wait for God to make His will perfectly clear, it was as if a great weight fell off him. He cried for joy. God used me to unburden and refocus his life.

We've asked many times for God to make His will clear, and He's always come through. So wait to act until God reveals His will to you, because too many Christians are outside the circle of His will, wondering why things aren't working out. He'll provide a clear vision for your future, but you need to wait patiently for God to provide His guidance.

### STEP TWO: OBEY GOD IMMEDIATELY.

Once God makes His will and timing clear to you, step out in faith. Obey. No matter how foolish or inconvenient it may seem, obey immediately and joyfully. I recently heard a testimony from a friend of mine who was told by the Lord to take a gallon of milk to a certain address in a less-than-reputable neighborhood. God actually gave him the street address. So he went online, printed point-to-point directions, stopped at a market to buy milk, drove to the house, and walked to the door. When he knocked, a Spanish speaking woman opened the door, grabbed the milk, and ran to her kitchen. My friend was turning to leave when a pre-teen came to the door and invited him in. Moments later, the mother came into the living room crying. She told my friend that she'd been praying for God to provide milk for her youngest child because she had no money and wouldn't be paid for a few more days.

I've heard many testimonies like this one.

God needs your help in bringing His Kingdom, love, forgiveness, and acceptance to our needy world. Are you ready for orders?

## Step Three: Expect God's Provision.

Finally, God will provide everything you need to do His will. He loves His kids. Let me give you a personal example.

Our daughter was born when I was in seminary. Our medical insurance had a $350 deductible. Since we lived from payday to payday, that was a huge debt to repay.

God tested us further. After our daughter came home from the hospital, she developed a condition requiring a second hospital stay and another deductible. Then we had $700 to pay. We prayed and prayed—but told no one but God about the need. Two weeks later, we received a check for $700—exactly what we needed. Some acquaintances sold land that they'd been trying to sell for a few years. God told them to mail us 10 percent of the $7,000 they received.

God is faithful to His faithful followers!

I have many more testimonies of God's provision I could share, but I encourage you to expect God to always provide what you need to do His will. Always!

## CONCLUSION

I hope you're ready to step into your destiny and follow God's leading wherever He takes you. He's absolutely faithful. You don't have to worry about provisions, but you must be very careful not to veer off course, act prematurely, and miss God's blessings. Fix your eyes on Him, and He'll provide all you need to do His will.

In the next chapter, you'll learn why God calls you to appreciate the joys of the moment and not be so concerned about what will happen in the future that you miss precious moments with Him.

### ENDNOTE

1. *Draper's Quick Quotes,* 5,226.

# CHAPTER 9

# Cherish God's Gift of Joy

*Though you have not seen [Jesus], you love Him; and even though you do not see Him now, you believe in Him and are filled with an inexpressible and glorious joy. —Apostle Peter* (1 Peter 1:8)

It's a bad world an incredibly bad world. But I have discovered in the midst of it a quiet and holy people who have learned a great secret. They have found a joy which is a thousand times better than any pleasure of our sinful life. They are despised and persecuted, but they care not. They are masters of their souls. They have overcome the world. These people are the Christians—and I am one of them. —The prayer of an anonymous third-century Christian anticipating martyrdom.

Sovereign joy buoys weary souls. It invades dark moments at Heaven's command and lifts drowning hearts above billowing crests of pain and sorrow. The One who lives in endless light is a Joy Giver. Our Father's heart is ever seeking those who look to Him for hope in the midst of darkness and despair. In love, He lifts His scepter, commanding Heaven's host to release joy in downcast human hearts.

My father died in 1981. The captain of my ship broke the news late one night while we were anchored in Athens Harbor.

I'd just returned from a brief tour of the ancient city when I was summoned to his cabin. After ushering me to a couch in his stateroom, he walked over to a small table and picked up a folded piece of paper.

After scanning the Red Cross message from my mom, he looked up and said, "Chaplain, I'm sorry to tell you that your father passed away."

I felt like someone punched me the stomach. I knew Dad was suffering from Lou Gehrig's disease—but I thought he had years to live since he was still working fulltime.

With tears streaming down my cheeks, I sobbed uncontrollably as my captain sat nearby handing me tissues. He even rubbed my back and offered me some water. Eventually, I composed myself, thanked him for caring so much, and went back to my stateroom. There I sat alone on my bunk, feeling like the world collapsed on me. Dad was dead.

A while later, my prayer partner stopped by; bad news travels quickly through a Navy ship. He prayed with and for me, we chatted, I cried some more—then God showed up. I felt His presence surround me like a bear hug.

Yes, God's tangible presence filled my room and soul. Rivers of tears still flowed, but they were now tears of joy. Real joy! I was filled with joy because Dad died *in Christ!* He was in Heaven feeling fine. No more having to endure an insensitive co-worker's ridicule about his slurred speech. No more worrying about suffocation or prolonged disability. At 54 years of age, he went home. He graduated from this life to Heaven and received his eternal reward.

*Sovereign joy!*

In the midst of gut-wrenching grief—joy! What a precious gift from our gracious God.

King David knew the darkness of despair and chronicled his experiences with God's joy. "Weeping may last through the night, but joy comes with the morning" (Ps. 30:5 NLT). "You turned my wailing into dancing; you removed my sackcloth and clothed me with joy" (Ps. 30:11).

I discovered that God's gift of joy comes at unexpected times, in unexpected ways. Its origin is Father God's loving heart. His joy visits us when things are good and bad, when we feel like celebrating, and when we're sad. Joy is God's gift to those who love Him. It's one of the "perks" that come with a surrendered life.

## THE WORLD NEEDS MORE JOY.

God wants you to stop striving so hard to find happiness. Joy is indestructible; happiness is like holding water in your hands—it quickly drains away. It's good while it lasts, but it doesn't last very long.

The word happy is found only 21 times in the 66 books of the New International Version of the Bible; happiness only six times. Joy is found 242 times, joyful 27 times, and joyfully 11 times. God's much more concerned with joy than happiness.

Almost everyone is happy when things go their way, but watch out when things don't go their way. I don't want to live for happiness because joy is much more substantive. Joy lasts; happiness doesn't. Joy sustains us in dark times; happiness is a good times thrill.

Christian joy is supernatural. It's a gift and a fruit of the Holy Spirit. It's poured into us and it also grows within us. It gets radically more delightful as it ripens.

It is so radical that the writer of Hebrews compliments his fellow first-century Christians by saying, "You sympathized with those in prison *and joyfully accepted the confiscation of your property*, because you knew that you yourselves had better and lasting possessions" (Heb. 10:34). Can you believe they were filled with joy because they were persecuted for their faith? Only God could make that happen.

God given joy blesses us in fair weather and during life's occasional storms. Happiness can't do that. That's because joy is everlasting, eternal, transforming. Happiness is fleeting. Reverend Dwight L. Moody tells us:

> Happiness is caused by things that happen around me, and circumstances will mar it; but joy flows right on through trouble; joy flows on through the dark; joy flows in the night as well as in the day; joy flows all through persecution and opposition. It is an unceasing fountain bubbling up in the heart; a secret spring the world can't see and doesn't know anything about. The Lord gives His people perpetual joy when they walk in obedience to Him.[1]

## WORRY WILL STEAL YOUR JOY.

Few things will steal your joy more quickly than worry. I know—I've battled worry most of my life. It wasn't until six years ago that worry's hold over me was broken after reading Dale Carnegie's book, *How to Stop Worrying and Start Living*. That was followed by a cleansing time of prayer, confession, and renouncement. I'm not totally free of worry, but it's significantly less troublesome and my life is more joyful than ever.

*So what is worry?*

To worry means to feel uneasy about some uncertain or threatening matter; to be troubled, fearful, or mentally and emotionally stressed or anxious.

Worry stresses your mind, emotions, and body. It can bring sickness or kill otherwise healthy people from heart attacks, ulcers, strokes, and a whole range of worry-induced and stress-related illnesses.

*Worry will rob you of joy, health, and long life!*

A recent survey asked a cross section of Americans to tell what worries them most. Let me summarize the findings:

- More than 70 percent said they worried about wasting too much time, especially watching TV.

- About 70 percent worried about not reading enough, not attending worship regularly, and not being active in community affairs.

- Twenty percent worried about personal debt and the same number about drinking too much.

Most of these joy-stealers can be eliminated by self-control. So confront your worries head on! Why? Because worry can literally wear you out! Sir John Lubbock says, "a day of worry is more exhausting than a day of work."[2] Worry affects our circulatory system, heart, glands, and our entire nervous system.

Jesus has a lot to say about worry because He knows how it negatively affects a human being's body, mind, emotions, and spiritual life. He commends you not to worry about anything since you're a child of a loving God who promises to meet your needs.

*Therefore I tell you, **do not worry about your life**, what you will eat or drink; or about your body, what you will wear. Is not life more important than food, and the body more important than clothes? Look at the birds of the air; they do not sow or reap or store away in barns, and yet your heavenly Father feeds them. Are you not much more valuable than they? Who of you by worrying can add a single hour to his life?*

*And **why do you worry about clothes**? See how the lilies of the field grow. They do not labor or spin. Yet I tell you that not even Solomon in all his splendor was dressed like one of these. If that is how God clothes the grass of the field, which is here today and tomorrow is thrown into the fire, will He not much more clothe you, O you of little* *faith? So do not worry, saying, 'What shall we eat?' or 'What shall we drink?' or 'What shall we wear?' For the pagans run after all these things, and your heavenly Father knows that you need them.* **But seek first His kingdom and His righteousness, and all these things will be given to you as well. Therefore do not worry about tomorrow, for tomorrow will worry about itself.** *Each day has enough trouble of its own* (Matthew 6:25-34).

Jesus teaches that worry is a waste of time and energy because Father God is in absolute control of the universe. Worry will significantly degrade your life and the lives of those you love.

So stop worrying about what you can't control and focus on what you can control—your reaction to life's challenges. Don't let the devil steal your joy by giving into the temptation to worry. You will worry less when you tap into God's power and love, and practice self-control.

Paul tells Timothy:

*God did not give us a spirit of timidity (of cowardice, of craven and cringing and fawning fear), but [He has given us a spirit] of power and of love and of calm and well-balanced mind and discipline and self-control* (2 Timothy 1:7 AMP).

This passage has so positively impacted my life that I developed, and twice facilitated for over 150 people, an entire weekend retreat based on this one verse. The positive impact on those who attended was amazing.

## STOP WORRYING AND START LIVING A JOYFUL LIFE.

Does worry still affect your quality of life? You're not alone if it does, because many Christians still worry. Like you, they need to confront worries head on by confessing worry as sin (a lack of faith in God's promises) and asking God for help in overcoming it. Why is worrying a sin? God's word says, "Trust in the Lord with all your heart and lean not on your own understanding; in all your ways acknowledge him, and he will make your paths straight" (Prov. 3:5-6). Not trusting in God's promises is a lack of faith in God's willingness to "make your paths straight." Whatever is not done in faith is sin (see Rom. 14:23). But that's not all; worry also negatively affects your health and relationships. That's never God's best life for you.

How can you get beyond a worry lifestyle and experience a joyful, worry-less life? The first step in your recovery from worry sickness is to give your whole life to Jesus. That means all you are, all you have, and all you hope to be. Everything there is to give. Lay it down at the foot of the cross.

Next, ask God to fill you with power to overcome worry. Claim Luke 11:13 and pray for God to fill you with His power every day. Jesus says, "If you then, though you are evil, know how to give good gifts to your children, how much more will your Father in heaven give the Holy Spirit to those who ask Him!" The Holy Spirit will empower you to live the Christian life with less worry.

Then, reprogram your thought patterns and actions by reading and claiming God's scriptural promises. Remember what I said in Chapter 2: *as you think, you feel, and as you feel, you act.* Thinking with a biblical perspective (trusting in your faithful Father God) will change your feelings (worry is a feeling you won't miss when it goes) and your actions (you won't feel worry affecting your decisions and actions).

Worry is a result of unsanctified habit patterns. It's rooted in a lack of faith in some area of your life. If you don't do something about it, you'll miss many opportunities for enjoying your life, and you may be too timid to take charge of your destiny.

I've summarized a strategy for overcoming worry in the Action Steps. But if worry persists after you put the action steps into practice, there could be generational issues, ungodly beliefs, soul/spirit hurts, or demonic oppression at the root of your worries.

If that's the case, you'd certainly benefit from receiving in-depth Christian counseling to help you break free from the root causes of worry, anxiety, shame, fear, and other lingering afflictions. If you have a deep issue to resolve, ask your pastor for counseling or for a referral to a licensed pastoral counselor.

## GOD WANTS YOU TO ENJOY YOUR LIFE

In preparation for writing this chapter, I journaled for over two weeks. Here's a short section from one of my conversations with God:

*You don't need to rush into the future; it will come quickly enough. Rest in the moment and see the beauty of life around you. Sky, trees, landscapes, mountains, oceans, clouds, birds. Observe the subtle variations of color in a sunrise, the rhythmic patterns of rain splashing in a puddle, the cry of a baby, the bark of a dog, the absence of noise in the night, your heartbeat, the miracle of sight. Appreciate good music, enjoy playing with children—so uninhibited, carefree, and at times, silly!*

*Sit by a quiet stream and look for trout, watch a leaf float by and get caught in the eddies, twisting and turning until it breaks free and continues its downstream journey.*

*My love is complete, unfettered, unbiased, joyous, expectant, uninhibited, encouraging, and wild. My purposes are grand, stretching, challenging, satisfying, rewarding, exciting, frightening, yet exhilarating.*

*Rest in My love. Don't fret about the future. Just rest in My love and enjoy each day as a precious gift. Rest your mind in the assurance of your bright future. Take precious moments to listen to My voice. I am calling you to quietude, rest, and peace. Don't let what could happen in the future keep you from enjoying what is happening in the moment. Rest in Me, and I will bring much joy to your life.*

God's guidance really helped me. I learned that one of the best ways to stop worrying about the future is to intentionally invest time enjoying the present. My wife and I are now in our mid-50s. We're not as spry as we once were—no more long hikes or bike rides through the mountains for us. Even though we're busy in ministry and getting older, we're still very intentional about seeing and appreciating the joy-giving things around us.

We enjoy gardens, birds, kayaking, traveling, swimming, walking—as well as all we do to keep ourselves spiritually fit. We make time to appreciate the moment and build precious memories. We don't worry much about the future anymore. We realized we can't control most of what's ahead, if anything, so we leave our worries in God's hands.

You can also break worry's power over your life and experience joy in little things every day. There will be hard times ahead but many wonderful times as well. With God's help, you'll see a significant improvement in your quality of life.

*Take Charge of Your Destiny*
*Principle Nine:*
*Don't be so concerned about the future*
*that you miss the joys of the moment.*

## ACTION STEPS

### STEP ONE: CONFESS YOUR WORRIES AS SIN.

Jesus says to you, "...do not worry about tomorrow, for tomorrow will worry about itself. Each day has enough trouble of its own" (Matt. 6:34).

In the early '80s, my wife and I attended a Christian conference at which the keynote speaker asked our gathering if anyone was struggling with worry. Hundreds of hands shot up, including mine. Then he said, "I want you to confess your sin of worry right now and ask God to forgive you." I was shocked to realize that worry is sin (it's actually a sinful thought pattern that evokes physiological responses like ulcers, high blood pressure, migraines, insomnia, colitis, heart attacks, strokes, etc.). I prayed for forgiveness, renounced my sin of worry, and asked God to help my faith grow. That was the beginning of my progressively more successful battle over worry.

*Faith displaces worry.*

As your faith grows, worry slowly but surely loses its power over you.

If you're worrying about something right now, take a minute to ask for God's forgiveness and assistance in growing in faith. Then pray using your God-given authority and command worry to leave you alone.

Here's a sample declarative prayer, "In the name of Jesus Christ I refuse to worry about _____ (add your concerns). I believe God will supply all my needs according to His riches in glory. Worry, leave me alone right now! I claim Philippians 4:6-7 for myself as a child of the Most High God. I will *not* be anxious about anything, but in everything, by prayer and petition, with thanksgiving, I present my requests to God. And the peace of God, which transcends all understanding, will guard my heart and my mind in Christ Jesus. Amen."

## STEP TWO: LIVE IN DAY-TIGHT COMPARTMENTS

Pilots have an uncanny ability to compartmentalize, as do race car drivers, professional athletes, and others in high-stress and dangerous occupations. When they're working, they focus only on their job. The smallest distraction could kill them and others. That's why they compartmentalize. You'll benefit from the same discipline. Learn to live one day at a time in day-tight compartments and stop worrying about tomorrow.

So what practical steps can you take to keep worry in check? There are too many to list, but let me give you a few practical examples.

For those overwhelmed by a major task, make a list of things you need to do to complete the task and prioritize them by due dates. Focus on the most critical tasks first. Do only what must be done each day and don't let the following day's tasks steal the present day's joy.

When I was studying full-time for my master's degree in theology, I found the huge workload manageable when I took an entire semester's requirements and divided them up into daily tasks. I had 5x8 card daily task lists for each week of the semester. Every day I assigned myself reading for each course, study time for exams, and research and writing time for papers. I had a set amount of work to do each day and when it was done, I stopped working. Some days I worked twelve hours and some six. My wife appreciated knowing when I was available to her as well. I didn't worry about cramming for exams or meeting writing deadlines because I chipped away daily at big assignments.

My boss, Senate Chaplain Barry Black, likes to say, "Life is hard by the yard, but it's a cinch by the inch." I certainly found that true in writing my doctoral dissertation as well as this book.

One last idea. If you find yourself worrying about mistakes you've made and their possible consequences, always ask yourself, "What's the worst thing that can happen to me?" That often puts things in perspective. Read Dale Carnegie's, *How to Stop Worrying and Start Living* for additional strategies for winning the war against worry!

## Conclusion

Joy is God's gift. He wants you to experience His joy in the midst of life's mountain peaks and valleys. Don't give into the temptation of believing God has abandoned you when things fall apart—He hasn't. Expect Him to make His presence known when you need Him most. He loves you and knows exactly what you need every day.

In the next chapter you'll learn why seeking God daily keeps you on course to your destiny. It's very easy to fall into religious routines that exclude God from your daily activities. When you do so, you may cut yourself off from His flow of grace, love, power, and wisdom. Your destiny is found in the center of His will. Seeking God daily keeps your relationship vibrant, your life focused on Kingdom service, and your future filled with adventures and victories.

### Endnotes

1. *Draper's Quick Quotes*, 6,529.
2. Ibid., 12,056.

# CHAPTER 10

# Keep Seeking God

*"Glory in His holy name; let the hearts of those who seek the Lord rejoice. Look to the Lord and His strength; seek His face always."—Ezra* (1 Chronicles 16:10-11)

"To have found God and still pursue him is the soul's paradox of love, scorned indeed by the too-easily-satisfied religionist, but justified in happy experience by the children of the burning heart."[1]
—A. W. Tozer

God is always ready to lend a hand. When I was on a flight from California to Hawaii, seated next to me was an insurance agent returning home from a business meeting. I introduced myself as a Navy chaplain. She said, "A chaplain? Is that like a minister?"

"Yes, I'm a minister."

"Can I ask you a question?"

"Go right ahead," I said.

"How can I find God?"

Having that question asked at the beginning of a six-hour flight is like a Christmas gift from Heaven. I knew God must have assigned our seats, so I prayed for guidance as the young lady began chatting about spiritual things. I soon shared the following verses:

*"For I know the plans I have for you," declares the Lord, "plans to prosper you and not to harm you, plans to give you hope and a future. Then you will call upon Me and come and pray to Me, and I will listen to you.* **You will seek Me and find Me when you seek Me with all your heart. I will be found by you,'** *declares the Lord* (Jeremiah 29:11-14).

We talked for over an hour. Just before the in-flight movie started, I said, "God really means what He says. Just ask Him to help you find Him, and He will."

When the movie ended, she got up to use the restroom. Upon her return, she looked at me with a smile and said, "I did it!"

That caught me off guard, but I finally mustered the courage to ask, "You did what?"

"I asked God to help me find Him!"

"Well you're in for an adventure! I'm really proud of you and so is Jesus."

My new friend committed herself to seeking God and He committed Himself to seeking her. When we parted, the newly committed seeker was well on her way to discovering Christ and gaining eternal life.

## WHAT'S AFTER SALVATION?

So what happens *after* someone accepts Jesus as his or her Lord and Savior and joins a local church? The rest of this chapter will answer the question, "Now what?" The reason this is an important question to me as a minister is quite simple. Until God opened my heart to the Gospel of the Kingdom I thought I knew the answer to the "Now what?" question.

Spiritual pilgrimage is a lifelong journey of faith. Following conversion, we need mature Christians to disciple us until we're grounded enough to disciple others. In evangelical churches, we're trained to share our faith and lead others to Christ. We're encouraged to "go on to maturity" so our walk with Jesus isn't hindered by the world, the flesh, or the devil. We worship regularly, tithe weekly, attend Sunday school and Bible studies, contribute our time and talents to God's work, and rejoice whenever new members join our ranks. Our faith life is mostly lived within our church buildings or members' homes, but occasionally we bring Jesus to the world. We're content with church life.

*Is that it, or is there more?*

Over the past decade I've come to realize that God didn't create His Church as an end in itself—an earthly organization for those who've professed Christ. God's church is much more than a safe haven where saints gather on Sundays. It's not a denomination, flawless doctrine, rules to follow, or a place of total agreement. We're the living Body of Christ.

God created His Church for the world. He created us to serve others in His name. We are the bearers of His Good News—the Gospel of the Kingdom of God.

Jesus tells us, "If anyone would come after Me, he must deny himself and take up his cross and follow Me. For whoever wants to save his life will lose it, but whoever loses his life for Me will find it" (Matt. 16:24-25).

We're called to invest ourselves in making the world a better place one life at a time. That applies to individuals and congregations, young and old, clergy and laity.

We're to invest ourselves in Kingdom service in seeking and saving the lost, healing the sick, and delivering the oppressed. The Church's mission is to do what Jesus did, and even more than He did (see John 14:12).

At its best, the Body of Christ is a spiritually empowered worship and discipleship community, where God heals deep wounds and empowers us to bring His Kingdom to a needy world.

As Jerry Cook tells us, "The Church is not supposed to replace the world as our field of Kingdom service. The Church is "people, equipped to serve, meeting needs everywhere in Jesus' name."[2] This tells me the Church is a movement, not a monument. It looks upward and outward, not inward. It's a community of God-seekers aiming their hearts toward Heaven and bringing hope to a needy world. It's imperfect people serving imperfect people, in the name of our perfect Savior.

The Church is about Jesus, not us. We're His Body. He's the boss. His world beckons.

We're not Baptists, Catholics, Pentecostals, or Methodists first and foremost. We're sons and daughters of the Most High God! We're one Body in Christ with many expressions. None of us has it all together, and our faith groups are not the only or best way to God.

We're fallible, redeemed people whose primary allegiance is to the One seated on Heaven's throne. It's all about King Jesus and His Kingdom.

Yes, God uses human institutions to do much good! There are tens of thousands of full-time Christian missionaries in the field right now, fully funded by their mission boards, praise God. However, many of us are separated by ideas that won't matter 100 years from now. We need to look beyond what separates us, bind our hearts together in Christian love, seek the Lord's direction, and make whatever sacrifices are necessary to combine forces and spread the Kingdom Gospel to the ends of the earth.

*We need each other to bring the Kingdom to earth for God's glory.*

There's only one body of Christ in the world, and we're individually members of it. Nothing we build in this world will endure. What lasts forever is our love for God and one another. We're Jesus' bride. God is preparing us for a great wedding feast and everlasting life! We ready ourselves for Heaven by loving others with Heaven's love—even if our doctrines clash, worship styles differ, and views on spiritual gifts remain poles apart—because we're going to Heaven *together*.

In May 1993, my wife organized the first of three annual March for Jesus events in Rhode Island. It was an incredible experience.

Picture this in your mind. Over 1,000 Christians of all ages, shapes, and colors from more than 40 different Catholic and Protestant churches, assemble in a small stadium and divide into five groups of about 200 each. Soon everyone begins a coordinated two-mile journey through downtown Newport waving flags, carrying thousands of balloons, wearing colorful tee shirts, and singing along with praise music playing on truck-mounted loudspeakers.

It was a Kingdom-focused event taking the walls off the Church. We could all agree that we were worshipping Jesus on the streets that day!

The following morning on the front page of our newspaper was this headline, *"Black and White, Young and Old, Catholic and Protestant…they all came together for one purpose: To praise Jesus."* Amen!

You're called to seek Jesus relentlessly, passionately, and earnestly. To pursue Him as a lover pursues a mate or as someone who finds a precious jewel in a field and makes any sacrifice to buy it. Seeking is an act of godly desperation.

You're called to a life of seeking God and making yourself available for His bidding. God willingly responds to your loving overtures with His undivided time and attention. You can pray anytime and know He hears you. But you have to seek Him with all your heart day by day. If you do, you'll surely find Him, not just once or twice in a lifetime or even once or twice in a week, but every time you seek Him with all your heart. He's waiting for you.

Isn't that amazing?

A.W. Tozer says, "We pursue God because, and only because, He has first put an urge within us that spurs us to the pursuit."[3] An urge—planted within your heart. An undeniable, unavoidable urge, a longing, desire, passion, and obsession compelling you to keep seeking the One who blesses you with the very desire spurring you on. Don't let anything keep you from pursuing God! You were created to know Him as deeply as you're willing to go.

## WHY DO SOME CHRISTIANS FALL AWAY?

It's disheartening to see once-zealous Christians fall away from Christ. Some decide that following Jesus is too much work. Others are obsessed with carnal pleasures. Then there are those too easily dissuaded in their quest for God by well-meaning but deceived friends and relatives.

Cognitive conversion—being convinced of good ideas about God—without a life-changing, supernatural encounter with God, like Pastor John Wesley's heartwarming Holy Spirit encounter at a Moravian prayer meeting, will rarely produce a sustainable commitment to Christ. Prior to his Holy Spirit encounter, John was a lackluster missionary preacher at best. Afterwards he became a mighty man of God. Here's how John describes his May 24, 1738, encounter with the Holy Spirit:

> In the evening I went very unwillingly to a society in Aldersgate Street, where one was reading Luther's preface to the Epistle to the Romans. About a quarter before nine, while the leader was describing the change which God works in the heart through faith in Christ, *I felt my heart strangely warmed*. I felt I did trust in Christ alone for salvation; and an assurance was given me that He had taken away my sins, even mine, and saved me from the law of sin and death (emphasis mine).[4]

From this experience until the end of his life, John saw thousands come to Christ through his preaching and teaching. He realized his destiny once he relinquished control of his life to the Spirit. You also need God's Spirit—the One who will warm your heart with Father God's loving presence—to guide, empower, and encourage you on your lifelong journey of faith.

Why? Satan is using his spiritual power against you. Unless you're filled daily with the Holy Spirit's power, you'll eventually dry up and maybe even give up. It's impossible to live a holy life without God's help. It's even harder to overcome an orphan spirit, critical nature, haughtiness, or other spiritually rooted hindrances to vibrant faith. Without the Spirit's assistance, you'll experience ebbing faith and unwillingness to seek and save the lost.

Jesus cautions us about unproductive faith in the parable of the seeds and the sower found in Matthew 13:1-23. There are four places where seed falls: on the path, on rocky places, among thorns, or on good soil. The seed stands for the Word of God sown in human hearts. The Kingdom message produces a bountiful harvest of souls, but only when the devil doesn't snatch it away. Jesus explains the Parable of the Sower, saying:

> *Listen then to what the parable of the sower means: When anyone hears the message about the kingdom and does not understand it, the evil one comes and snatches away what was sown in his heart. This is the seed sown along the path. The one who received the seed that fell on rocky places is the man who hears the word and at once receives it with joy. But since he has no root, he lasts only a short time. When trouble or persecution comes because of the word, he quickly falls away. The one who received the seed that fell among the thorns is the man who hears the word, but the worries of this life and the deceitfulness of wealth choke it, making it unfruitful. But the one who received the seed*

*that fell on good soil is the man who hears the word and understands it. He produces a crop, yielding a hundred, sixty or thirty times what was sown* (Matthew 13:18-23).

You can't allow passivity, trouble, persecution, the worries of this life, or the deceitfulness of wealth choke your faith to death. You have to receive, and keep receiving day after day, the heart-warming presence of God's Spirit to succeed in living for God's glory. Only then will you produce a crop, yielding a hundred, sixty, or thirty times what the Holy Spirit has sown in your life.

## HELP IS ON THE WAY!

The world is in trouble, but help is on the way. God's international army is gearing up for another great spiritual battle. Multitudes from around our nation and across the world are committing their time, talents, and treasure in a quest for souls, a harvest of epic proportions, a worldwide outreach effort. How do we know? Look at worldwide trends—the wind of God is blowing with increasing intensity. The distance from Heaven to our hearts is diminishing. The five-fold ministries have been reinstated in the church (see Eph. 4:11). There's an open Heaven over many ministries; angels are appearing more frequently; signs and wonders are increasing. A great harvest of souls is already spreading across many nations and will soon sweep the world.

The Lord is moving in accelerated outpourings of the Holy Spirit. Let me give you an example. Not long ago, the Senate Chaplain told me that in 2005 more people came to Christ through Billy Graham's ministry than in all previous years of his ministry combined. Over 1,000,000 souls gave their hearts to Jesus in India alone.[5]

In Mozambique, Roland and Heidi Baker have witnessed more than 1,000,000 souls saved and 6,500 churches opened in the past 18 years. Leif Hetland has seen more than 500,000 come to Christ in Pakistan. Yoido Full Gospel church in Seoul, Korea, has exceeded 1,000,000 members committed to sacrificial giving, hours of daily intercession, in-depth Bible study, and evangelism at home and abroad.

Millions are giving their hearts to Jesus in China, Brazil, Uganda, Kenya, and many other nations. Jesus is appearing to Muslims in dreams and visions, and they're sovereignly converted. Many non-Western nations are sending missionaries to Western nations.

I pray that soon revival fire will spread to Western nations, but as I said in the last chapter, it may take a season of protracted difficulty to get our nation's attention and turn us back to Christ. Is your church ready to receive hundreds of converts? If not, get ready!

## We Must Pursue God if We Hope To Win the World for Christ.

We'll only reverse the Western church's negative trends and help those we love keep seeking God if we keep Heaven in view. It's our responsibility to seek and save the lost by seeking God's face daily, receiving our marching orders, and going out to the highways and byways to invite the lost into His Kingdom.

In Springfield, Virginia, where I lead English ministry at International Calvary Church, there are over 5,000 Spanish speakers within one mile of our facility. We prayed many months for a way to reach them for Christ. God answered our prayers by sending us a talented, Spirit-filled Spanish pastor and his family, along with two other anointed Spanish-speaking families. Recently, these Kingdom-minded saints made contact with 1,000 Spanish speakers in our neighborhood by passing out flyers for our inaugural Spanish service. They are now warmly received as they prayer-walk and witness in our neighborhood. In less than a year, over 40 Spanish-speaking neighbors have joined our church.

I challenge you to earnestly seek God's will for your church.

God rewards those who earnestly seek Him (Heb. 11:6). You're not smart enough to know God's specific will for your life or church without continually seeking His counsel. Seek His guidance so that what He tells you and you will bring His Kingdom to earth.

## God Really Is on Your Side.

You'll have a very bright future if you commit to seeking God daily. He's preparing you for progressively more effective Kingdom service. So, take heart; you're not in the battle alone. Fix your eyes on Jesus and trust Him to guide you day by day. The Holy Spirit etched the message below on my heart as I was praying about God's will for the body of Christ in Western churches.

As I was journaling ideas on what a "seeker's" life is all about, I received this word from the Lord.

> *I desire for my children to know Me, not just about Me. I am jealous of their distractions. I am calling My Church to sanctified life, but even more to Spirit-filled, victorious living, progressively more decisive engagement with Me, and significantly more intimacy with Me.*

> *Tell My people the sun is rising. Darkness is being rooted out. I am coming to purge the dross from my Church. No more lackluster commitments. I want mobilized forces for good.*

> *Arise and shine, for My glory is upon you. Wake up, sleepers, and prepare your lives for battle. I am calling you out of your precious buildings into the streets. Get out of your*

*comfortable sanctuaries into the mission fields of your own neighborhoods, businesses, campuses, bases, offices, and worksites.*

*Arise and shine. Give Me the glory. I am coming to anoint all who call upon My name and surrender to My purposes.*

*Don't miss opportunities to flow in the river of My love, power, and peace. I am coming in a mighty wind to call out My chosen ones. No more easy religion. No more passive lives of faith. No! I desire accelerated lives, anointed lives, Kingdom-focused lives filled with sovereign joy, peace, and love.*

*Mobilize—prepare for revival. Throw open your hearts to Me. Seek My face and I will guide you in the days to come.*

*I am coming in the wind. I am coming to My people. Prepare for harvest—I am coming.*

*Take Charge of Your Destiny*
*Principle Ten:*
*Seek God and you will find Him;*
*He's waiting for you.*

## ACTION STEPS

### STEP ONE: SEEK GOD DAILY.

*Paul says, "Do you not know that your body is a temple of the Holy Spirit, who is in you, whom you have received from God? You are not your own; you were bought at a price. Therefore honor God with your body"* (1 Corinthians 6:19-20).

You don't belong to yourself anymore. When Jesus bought you back from sin with His blood, you became His disciple and more. He cherishes you as His co-heir and treats you accordingly. He deserves your gratitude, loyalty, and attention, and promises to be with you forever. Seek Him and you will find Him. Seek Him throughout the day and you will stay in His presence. He wants you to take charge of your destiny as you follow His plans for your life.

Let God's Word dwell in you richly and produce a harvest of righteousness. Pray often, fast frequently, eliminate unnecessary distractions from your life, and trust God to show you His plans to prosper you and not to harm you, plans to give you hope and a future (see Jer. 29:11).

### STEP TWO: GUARD YOUR DESTINY.

Esau sold his birthright for a bowl of lentil stew. Some Christians are giving away their destinies for the sake of comfort, convenience, and pleasure. Don't join their ranks. Work out your salvation with praise and thanksgiving. You have everything to gain by yielding your future to Jesus and fulfilling your destiny!

Let me give you something to think about. Every Sunday our congregation shouts the following affirmation. It's a declaration of God's promises in modern parlance. One of our members recently told me that in a time of great temptation he started reciting this declaration from memory and the tempter fled. Perhaps when you're tempted to give up seeking God, you can find strength in the assurance these words bring us. Let this be your declaration as well.

**I am a Child of the Most High God.**
**The devil has lost me.**
**Jesus has redeemed me.**
**The Holy Spirit empowers me.**
**The Word of God guides me.**
**Heaven awaits me.**
**I am a Child of the Most High God.**

Live like a child of the Most High God and you won't miss your destiny.

### STEP THREE: PRACTICE SELF CONTROL.

Proverbs 25:28 says, *"Like a city whose walls are broken down is a man who lacks self-control."* Self-control is a fruit of the Spirit. It ripens over time but must be carefully cultivated. Paul cautions you about self-seeking:

> *To those who by persistence in doing good seek glory, honor and immortality, He will give eternal life. But for those who are self-seeking and who reject the truth and follow evil, there will be wrath and anger* (Romans 2:7-8).

Do whatever it takes to keep your life pure, focused on Heaven, and available to God. Stay pure by creating boundaries that safeguard your integrity. Fix your thoughts on Jesus (see Heb. 3:1). Surrender your life daily to God and expect Him to employ you in Kingdom service. He will equip you for anything He calls you to do.

## CONCLUSION

The Lord is calling you to a life of seeking. He's available 24/7. So let seeking Him be the focus of your life, and you'll experience His presence and blessings in ways others only dream of. You'll see your heart filled with love and joy, your family life energized and heaven-focused, and many come into the Kingdom as the Holy Spirit leads you to those seeking Christ as their Savior.

In the next chapter you'll see why embracing humility and letting others help you leads to fulfilling your destiny. Christianity is a team sport. You won't live it well in prideful isolation.

### ENDNOTES

1. A.W. Tozer, *The Pursuit of God* (Camp Hill: Christian Publications, Inc., 1982), 15.

2. Jerry Cook, *Love, Acceptance, and Forgiveness: Equipping the Church to be Truly Christian in a Non-Christian World* (Ventura: Regal Books, 1979), 45.

3. *Draper's Quotes*, 9,218.

4. John Wesley's Journal, vol vi.ii.xvi, "I Felt My Heart Strangely Warmed," Christian Ethereal Library, http://www.ccel.org/ccel/wesley/journal.vi.ii.xvi.html.

5. Discussion between Dr. Barry Black and Rev. Franklin Graham at Nelson Books' spring 2006 authors' meeting.

CHAPTER 11

# Embrace Humility

*"The pride of your heart has deceived you...Though you soar like the eagle and make your nest among the stars; from there I will bring you down," declares the Lord. ... Oh, what a disaster awaits you. —Obadiah's prophecy just prior to the fall of Jerusalem in 586 B.C. (Obad. 1:3-5).*

The essential vice, the utmost evil, is pride. Unchastity, anger, greed, drunkenness, and all that, are mere fleabites in comparison. It was through pride that the devil became the devil. Pride leads to every other vice; it is the complete anti-God state of mind. —C.S. Lewis

Pride is a dangerous bedfellow, an enemy of God. It leads us into dark places.

King David says, "Love the Lord, all His saints! The Lord preserves the faithful, but the proud He pays back in full" (Ps. 31: 23), and "Men of perverse heart shall be far from Me; I will have nothing to do with evil. ...whoever has haughty eyes and a proud heart, him will I not endure" (Ps. 101:4-5). King Solomon adds, "When pride comes, then comes disgrace" (Prov. 11:2).

*God hates pride because it exalts itself at the expense of others.*

In the early '90s, my family and I were stationed in Jacksonville, North Carolina. Since I wasn't assigned to a military chapel, we attended a 400+ member Baptist church near our home so we could meet people from the community. After a few months, I made an appointment to see the pastor. He was around my age and about a year into his pastorate. I offered to assist in teaching a Sunday school class or in any other way he thought I could help. As I was offering my services, he was unconsciously shaking his head, expressing the real sentiment of his heart. "No, thanks," was written in his body language. He abruptly ended our conversation and escorted me to the door. We chose to worship with another congregation. He resigned a year later.

Whatever drove this pastor away may have originated in his unwillingness to let others help him. God calls that pride. Every pastor needs trusted assistants to co-labor in meeting a congregation's needs. Lone rangers don't last long in ministry—they burn out or wear out because they isolate themselves from friendship and accountability. Whether it's fear of failure or a controlling spirit, those who refuse assistance don't last long in one place. Pride takes them out and inflicts on their congregations much emotional and spiritual upheaval. It takes many months for a church to recover when their spiritual leader unexpectedly abandons ship.

Pride undermines the advancement of God's Kingdom, while humility often leads to cooperative ministry ventures and the rapid advancement of God's Kingdom.

In 2005, over 400 Washington DC-area churches joined together in supporting the Luis Palau Festival held on the National Mall. Thousands accepted Jesus as their Savior. As the event neared, scores of churches from outside the 495 beltway banded together in renovating a dozen Washington DC public schools. Many of those affected by these cooperative ventures also attended the festival and gave their hearts to Jesus.

Following the festival, hundreds of the same churches formed a cooperative alliance called *Power to Change, DC*, which focuses on renewing social and educational infrastructures. Millions of dollars in donations are flowing into our nation's capitol in an effort to take back what the devil has stolen from God's people.

What will make this effort successful is not the brilliance of its leadership, but the humility of its leaders. No individuals are seeking glory. When no one cares who gets the credit, anything is possible.

## THE DESTRUCTIVE POWER OF PRIDE

Richard Baxter tells us:

Pride is a vice that ill suits those that would lead others in a humble way to Heaven. Let us take heed, lest when we have brought others so far, the gates should prove too narrow for ourselves. For God, who thrust out a proud angel, will not tolerate a proud preacher, either. For it is pride that is at the root of all other sins: envy, contention, discontent, and all hindrances that would prevent renewal. Where there is pride, all want to lead and none want to follow or to agree.[1]

Pride was the devil's downfall. He lusted for His Creator's place on the throne. God judged him and consigned him to a finite existence within the bounds of earth. Listen to what Isaiah says about the devil's fall from grace.

*How you have fallen from heaven, O morning star, son of the dawn! You have been cast down to the earth, you who once laid low the nations! You said in your heart, "I will ascend to heaven; I will raise my throne above the stars of God; I will sit enthroned on the mount of assembly, on the utmost heights of the sacred mountain. I will ascend above the tops of the clouds; I will make myself like the Most High"* (Isaiah 14:12-14).

The enemy's end is sure. Pride comes before a fall and in the devil's case his long fall from the throne room of God will come to an end in a fiery pit. As Richard Newton says, "Let me give you the history of pride in three small chapters. The beginning of pride was in Heaven. The continuance of pride is on earth. The end of pride is in hell. This history shows how unprofitable it is."[2]

*Pride leads to a host of sins.*

A decade ago, I ministered to a woman whose life was almost ruined because she was too embarrassed to seek help. I had no idea how tormented she was when she came forward for prayer following a service at which I was the guest preacher. After placing my hands on her face and closing my eyes, I saw a vision of a '60s-style living room. Seated playing a large upright piano was a young girl about nine or ten years old. At the near end of the piano, watching the pianist, was a 6- or 7-year-old girl. She was wearing a frilly white dress, shiny black shoes, and standing by an open window.

I told the woman what I was seeing, and she told me I was describing her family's living room. I asked if she were the one playing the piano or watching the pianist. She said she was the observer. That's when the Holy Spirit told me that a spirit of resentment entered her at the moment in time pictured in my vision. So I asked her if she resented her sister for the affirmation her mother lavished on her for playing the piano. She said yes, admitted hating her sister, and confessed to daily inner torment since childhood. I led her in confessing the sins of resentment, self-hatred, and despising her sister and mother. With no legal toehold to hang onto, the oppressive spirit left without a fight.

How was she released from her tormentor?

Overwhelming desperation resulted in the woman swallowing her pride and coming forward to see if God would help her. He did! He showed me the start of her affliction—the exact moment when a gateway opened in her heart and a spirit of resentment rushed in. Then the Holy Spirit delivered her from a lifetime of inner turmoil and self-condemnation. She felt immediate relief.

Following our brief encounter, she wept with thanksgiving for her newfound freedom. Humble desperation brought her to me, the Holy Spirit revealed the genesis of her problem, and then God's power gently evicted the malevolent spirit. She wanted to die as she was walking forward, but moments later her sins were forgiven, God's love filled her heart, and she was free to take charge of her destiny. All because she humbled herself and sought relief for her troubled heart.

*God rewards humility.*

Don't let pride ruin your life. Its power to injure you and those around you is greater than you can overcome on your own. Jesus calls you to love others with His love. Pride won't let you love like He does. So if you're struggling with pride, ask God to show you its root cause.

In case you don't know what God says about the downside of pride:

HERE'S A BRIEF LIST OF PRIDE'S NEGATIVE CONSEQUENCES:

- Pride keeps people from seeking God (see Ps. 10:4).

- Pride leads to arrogance (see Ps. 31:18).

- Pride leads to slander (see Ps. 56:2).

- Pride leads to lying (see Ps. 59:12).

- Pride brings disgrace (see Prov. 11:2).

- Pride leads to quarrels (see Prov. 13:10).

- Pride can destroy a family (see Prov. 15:25).

- Pride leads to destruction (see Prov. 16:18).

- Pride brings God's judgment (see Isa. 10:23).

- Pride brings destruction to nations (see Ezek. 32:12).

## WHAT GOD SAYS ABOUT PRIDE IN HIS CHURCH

As I was praying about the focus of this chapter, the Lord was pouring His Spirit into me in amazing ways. It's truly been a mountaintop experience. As I was journaling about the down side of pride, the Lord opened my eyes to a fresh view of its destructive power.

The Lord asks us:

*Do you understand why pride is so destructive? It tears down walls of trust and brings pain to its victims. Pride is a spiritual force wreaking havoc in the hearts of billions. It clouds judgment, brings great pain to families, separates wounded hearts, and breaks apart marriages.*

*I grieve to see the power that pride has in My church. It is a curse that separates My children from one another. It inflicts wounds so deep that many victims never recover. How? Through unforgiveness, haughtiness, spiritual arrogance, unwillingness to admit deep needs, failure to confess sin. A deep rift comes between My people and My heart when they are unwilling to humble themselves before Me. That cuts them off from the flow of my grace. That gives satan a foothold that he exploits against My people. It sets a tone of competition where there should be cooperation. It leaves a trail of victims so long it can't be counted.*

*Humility is the way to absolute freedom. If My people will humble themselves and confess their many sins, I will forgive them and set them on course to their destiny. Too many supposed "saints" are strongholds of pride. They think their ideas of Me lead to eternity. They are wrong—only My forgiveness opens the door to eternal life.*

*Follow My example—let go of your need for control. Allow Me to lead your life—let Me heal your wounds and fill you with my love, joy, and peace.*

*If My people will only come to Me in humility, I will bless them with unfolding and unfailing plans for their future.*

## THE POSITIVE POWER OF HUMILITY

Humility is the key to absolute freedom. Its sweet fragrance draws human hearts to Jesus. Humility also produces gentleness of spirit and passion to serve others. It refreshes rather than oppresses and binds hearts together in love. It's the polar opposite of pride and an essential attribute of *agape*. As First Corinthians 13:4 tells us, "Love is patient, love is kind. It does not envy, it does not boast, *it is **not** proud*."

Listen to what Apostle Paul also says about humility:

*As a prisoner for the Lord, then, I urge you to live a life worthy of the calling you have received. **Be completely humble and gentle; be patient, bearing with one another in love.** Make every effort **to keep the unity of the Spirit through the bond of peace.** There is one body and one Spirit—just as you were called to one hope when you were called—one Lord, one faith, one baptism; one God and Father of all, who is over all and through all and in all"* (Ephesians 4:1-6).

Notice that Paul lists a series of Christian attributes and attitudes. Christ-like character builds up Jesus' body and furthers His Kingdom. Living your life worthy of your calling is living like the Lord and for the Lord. It's seeing the world and the body of Christ as He sees them—through loving, compassionate, expectant eyes.

Jesus knows when His Kingdom will come in all its glory. Your part in bringing His Kingdom to earth is optimized when you allow Jesus to remove anything hindering your complete surrender to Him. That's humility in action.

*Humility grows as pride dies.*

John the Baptist said about Jesus, "He must become greater; I must become less" (John 3:30). Paul says of himself, "I have been crucified with Christ and I no longer live, but Christ lives in me. The life I live in the body, I live by faith in the Son of God, who loved me and gave Himself for me" (Gal. 2:20).

You could sum up their humble attitudes in a simple prayer, "Less of me, Lord, and more of You!" That's humility. That's Kingdom-building power at work. John was the Messiah's herald. Paul wrote the most New Testament books, evangelized the Gentile world, saw amazing miracles in his decades of evangelistic ministry, and died a martyr's death. Paul's humility equipped him to bring God's Kingdom to earth one heart at a time.

*No matter how you try to justify it, pride is **always** a sin.*

Humility, however, is a positive Kingdom-building fruit of the Spirit's purifying work in a human heart. Pride breaks hearts; humility heals them. Humility is a force to be reckoned with in a prideful world. Its power to change the world is limitless.

Here's a brief list of humility's positive consequences:

- Humility brings wisdom (Prov. 11:2).
- Humility brings honor (Prov. 15:33).
- Humility brings wealth (Prov. 22:4).
- Humility brings God's guidance (Ps.25:9).
- Humility brings God's crown of salvation (Ps. 149:4).
- Humility brings God's grace (Prov.3:34).
- Humility brings God's esteem (Isa. 66:2).

- Humility brings shelter from God's wrath (Zeph. 2:3).

- Humility brings God's provision in times of need (Ps. 147:6).

- Humility brings God's affirmation and esteem (Luke 18:14).

Once again we turn to Apostle Paul's insights on Kingdom life. He understood what it means to die to self in order to live for God's glory in bringing His Kingdom to earth. He writes:

*Since, then, you have been raised with Christ, set your hearts on things above, where Christ is seated at the right hand of God. Set your minds on things above, not on earthly things. For you died, and your life is now hidden with Christ in God. When Christ, who is your life, appears, then you also will appear with Him in glory. Put to death, therefore, whatever belongs to your earthly nature* (Colossians 3:1-5).

You should set your heart and mind on things above instead of on earthly things (see Col. 3:1-2). That's because Heaven is where Jesus reigns and where His power to change the world originates.

Peter's admonition echoes Paul's thoughts,

*Finally, all of you, live in harmony with one another; be sympathetic, love as brothers, **be compassionate and humble**. Do not repay evil with evil or insult with insult, but with blessing, because to this you were called so that you may inherit a blessing* (1 Peter 3:8-9).

Peter advises future leaders in saying,

*Likewise, you who are younger, be subject to the elders. Clothe yourselves, all of you, **with humility toward one*** *another, for "God opposes the proud but gives grace to the humble." Humble yourselves, therefore, under the mighty hand of God so that at the proper time He may exalt you, casting all your anxieties on Him, because He cares for you. Be sober-minded; be watchful. Your adversary the devil prowls around like a roaring lion, seeking someone to devour* (1 Peter 5:5-8 ESV).

Humility was lacking in the leaders of Jesus' day. One Sabbath, He was invited to the home of an influential Pharisee. Spies were looking for a way to accuse Jesus. Following a brief exchange on the lawfulness of healing on the Sabbath, Jesus began to observe His fellow dinner guests. He discovered a disheartening truth about Israel's leaders—one He felt needed to be confronted. Luke tells us:

*When He noticed how the guests picked the places of honor at the table, He told them this parable: "When someone invites you to a wedding feast, **do not take the place of honor,** for a person more distinguished than you may have been invited. If so, the host who invited both of you will come and say to you, 'Give this man your seat.' Then, humiliated, you will have to take the least important place. But when you are invited, take the lowest place, so that when your host comes, he will say to you, 'Friend, move up to a better place.' Then you will be honored in the presence of all your fellow guests. **For everyone who exalts himself will be humbled, and he who humbles himself will be exalted"** (Luke 14:7-11).*

We need each other's help in living victorious Christian lives. We can't do everything ourselves and expect to bring in God's Kingdom. We need to team up, encourage one another, and prayerfully ask God to bless our combined efforts with a generous anointing of the Holy Spirit.

*Take Charge of Your Destiny*
*Principle Eleven:*
*Don't try to do everything by yourself;*
*let others help you.*

## ACTION STEPS

### STEP ONE: HUMBLY ASK FOR FORGIVENESS.

A true servant of God has a humble heart. Pride, on the other hand, will taint your view of reality and siphon off your spiritual power. If you sense pride gaining a foothold in your heart, it's essential that you ask God for help in overcoming it. Take heed of what Solomon says, "Pride ends in humiliation, while humility brings honor" (Prov. 29:23 NLT).

Apostle John promises that if you confess your sins, God is faithful and just and will forgive your sins and purify you of all unrighteousness (see 1 John 1:9). Humbly confessing your sins to God will free you from pride's grip and keep you on course to your destiny.

Part two of this action step is to ask for forgiveness from everyone you've hurt. Initially it may take you a while to do this, but it's essential for your spiritual growth. If you have issues with someone who has already passed away, write a letter to him or her and confess what you did wrong. Then pray over the letter and shred it.

One caution: If something you did in secret would do harm to someone if it's brought up, just ask God to forgive you and let it go. If you can make amends in a positive way that builds up relationships, go ahead and do so.

### STEP TWO: HUMBLY OFFER FORGIVENESS.

If someone has taken advantage of you by not repaying a debt or fulfilling a promise and there's no hope it will happen, let it go. I had to do that three decades ago when a "friend" purchased books from me and never paid me for them. I finally wrote him a letter and cancelled the debt. That took away the devil's foothold and immediately freed me from resentment and self-righteous indignation. I slept much better that night.

Here's the tough one. If you've been hurt by someone and haven't dealt with it, you could still be negatively affected years after the incident. To overcome abuse, abandonment, and other emotionally debilitating experiences usually requires deep inner healing. If this is the case, you will benefit from in-depth counseling from your pastor.

## STEP THREE: ASK OTHERS TO HELP YOU.

Military service teaches teamwork. A Marine Corps fire team optimizes each member's skills for the common good. Together they're a formidable force. It's much the same in Christian service. Jesus sent his men out two by two for a reason. They encouraged and prayed for one another. Teams usually perform more effectively than lone rangers or groups of individuals.

Don't let pride keep you from asking for help with anything hindering your spiritual life and ministry. You won't regret it!

## Conclusion

Prideful loners rarely make effective leaders. They live in isolation, have little if any accountability, and often become heavy handed with those closest to them. Bringing God's Kingdom to earth requires teamwork. It increases the talent and gift pool and creates synergy that motivates everyone to higher standards of integrity and service. If you humble yourself and follow God's plan for your life, you'll bring His Kingdom to earth one heart at a time.

Life often brings great burdens to bear. Without God's help, the load can crush our spirits and neutralize our witness. In the next chapter, I'll discuss the importance of leaning into Jesus and letting Him carry your burdens.

### Endnote

1. "The Reformed Pastor," *Christianity Today,* Vol. 40, no. 9.

CHAPTER 12

# Release Your Burdens

*My soul finds rest in God alone; my salvation comes from Him. He alone is my rock and my salvation; He is my fortress, I will never be shaken....Find rest, O my soul, in God alone; my hope comes from Him. —King David* (Psalm 62:1-2, 5)

To every toiling, heavy-laden sinner, Jesus says, "Come to me and rest." But there are many toiling, heavy-laden believers, too. For them this same invitation is meant. Note well the words of Jesus, if you are heavy-laden with your service, and do not mistake it. It is not, "Go, labor on," as perhaps you imagine. On the contrary, it is stop, turn back, "Come to me and rest." Never, never did Christ send a heavy-laden one to work; never, never did He send a hungry one, a weary one, a sick or sorrowing one, away on any service. For such the Bible only says, "Come, come, come." —Hudson Taylor (Founder of the Inland China Mission)

Jesus is your burden bearer. He took your sins to Calvary, bearing the full weight of God's wrath on your behalf. His cross, shed blood, death, and resurrection changed everything! Heaven's doors opened to all who embrace Jesus as their Savior. No more fear of death or judgment. You have new life.

Everlasting life. New life brings rest—glorious, undeserved, rapturous rest—for weary souls.

## How to Deal with Your Burdens

Are you feeling the burden of guilt, loss, sickness, failure, or rejection? Is your mind weighed down by past mistakes or current squabbles? Do you have physical disabilities that make life difficult or painful? Then let God share your burdens. You weren't meant to carry them alone. That's right! Solo burden bearing isn't God's best for your life. So why not let Jesus bear your burdens and experience His rest for your soul?

When I was stationed in Virginia Beach, a young sailor came to me for counseling. He immediately started complaining about his parents, the Navy, and other things. He kept rambling on about everyone's insensitivity to his needs. While I was listening, the Holy Spirit brought two unexpected words to my mind—*horrendous nightmares*.

How odd, I thought, this must be God because I'd never come up with that thought.

So I said, "When are we going to talk about your horrendous nightmares?"

"How do you know about that?"

"God just told me; so why don't you tell me about your nightmares?"

"Well, Chaplain, when I was sixteen, my girlfriend dumped me, so I went into the woods and prayed to the devil to get her back. That's when something invisible tackled me, threw me to the ground, and started choking me. I cried out to God for help and the thing went away, but since then I've had terrible nightmares."

"You prayed to the devil? What were you thinking?"

"I was desperate!"

He was desperate *and* foolish.

I asked if I could pray for him. Twenty minutes later the source of his horrendous nightmares was gone and his life was surrendered to Jesus. Yes, he'd prayed to the devil and suffered hell's fury for six years as a result. He was led to me and set free through the power of the Holy Spirit, the authority of God's Word, and his confession of a host of sins related to what began as innocent dabbling in witchcraft.

God delivered him from the devil's grip because He sincerely wanted help.

What a gracious God we serve. He'll even redeem those who've worshipped the devil himself.

That's *agape* in action.

Not long ago my wife and I were on retreat for two weeks in North Carolina. I was there to work on this book while Sally was attending the first training module of Restoring the Foundations Ministry. Along with counseling protocols, a main focus of her introductory course was helping students release their burdens of sin and ungodly beliefs in preparation for assisting future counselees to release their burdens. It was amazing to see how many students at the graduation banquet gave testimonies of God freeing them from life-long struggles through the power of the Holy Spirit, prayer, and the Word of God.

Tears flowed unashamedly from teens and seniors alike.

God lifted a great weight from their weary souls. Their newfound freedom is a testimony of God's willingness to free us from anything hindering our spiritual growth. That day, twenty-nine liberated graduates were commissioned to set other captives free.

When you release *your* burdens, you'll also be more effective in helping others get rid of theirs. Are you willing to let Jesus take your burdens? You can rely on Him because He's the ultimate burden bearer. He'll empower you to set captives free and bring His Kingdom to Earth.

How does that work? In a case like that of the nightmare-plagued sailor mentioned above, Jesus says, *"...if I drive out demons by the Spirit of God, then the Kingdom of God has come upon you"* (Matt. 12:28). A young man was plagued by terrifying dreams for six years. He feared sleep. His life was hell. He sought help and was released from his burden by the power of the Holy Spirit! He was finally able to rest in God's love.

It's that simple.

I asked him to confess his sins related to worshiping the devil and his involvement in witchcraft. Then I claimed the Scriptures dealing with a Christian's spiritual authority over demonic oppression, ordered the intruder to leave in Jesus' name, and the dark spirit relinquished its foothold in the young man's mind and emotions. Then my counselee prayed to receive Jesus as his Savior and the Holy Spirit filled his heart. God transformed him in less than an hour.

No matter what's burdening you, God can set you free. He doesn't want you carrying around anything that hinders your spiritual life, relationships, or ministry.

That's right! He doesn't want you weighed down by burdens you can release with His help. He's willing to remove many types of burdens and help you bear the ones He can't remove, like the deaths of loved ones, ongoing trials, or past mistakes.

What He will do in *every* case is progressively help you find peace and rest following a terrible tragedy, rejection, or traumatic injury. Even after years of frustration and failure, there can be a new day, another chance, and an unexpected, but much appreciated, victory!

That's because Jesus is your burden bearer.

He's the one who created you, redeemed you, and loves you unconditionally. He knows who you will become with His help. He's calling you to release your burdens so you can help others release their burdens and bring His Kingdom to earth one heart at a time.

So let's look at what the Bible says about letting go of your burdens and experiencing rest for your soul.

## WHAT THE OLD TESTAMENT TEACHES ABOUT GOD'S REST

Sabbath observance is a main focus of Old Testament teachings on rest. It's God's basic provision for taking care of yourself so your body, mind, and spirit stay as healthy as possible, for as long as possible. God wants you to rest so you don't burn out from ceaseless toil.

He's so serious about the need for His people to rest that He includes Sabbath observance in His top Ten Commandments. The fourth one says,

> *Six days you shall labor and do all your work, but **the seventh day is a Sabbath to the Lord your God. On it you shall not do any work**, neither you, nor your son or daughter, nor your manservant or maidservant, nor your animals, nor the alien within your gates. For in six days the Lord made the heavens and the earth, the sea, and all that is in them, but he rested on the seventh day. Therefore the Lord blessed the Sabbath day and made it holy* (Exodus 20: 9-11).

Rev. Henry Ward Beecher says, "A world without a Sabbath would be like a man without a smile, like a summer without flowers, and like a homestead without a garden. It is the most joyous day of the whole week."[1] Why would he say that?

You weren't made to work seven days a week without rest or to carry life's burdens without God's help. That's one reason God created the Sabbath. It's a day for renewing your mind, body, and spirit and refocusing on what's most important—your relationship with the Lord! Sabbath is a day for rest, renewal, and reestablishing your priorities. God's serious about you resting at least one day a week.

But what if you must work on the Sabbath? Find another day to rest your mind, will, and emotions—and recharge your spiritual batteries. You'll live a much more meaningful life if you take the time to rest! Why? Because...

*Working seven days a week without a break will eventually break you!*

Make time to rest your body and mind at least one day a week. Your life will be much more fruitful in the long-run if you do. So, take Sabbath rest seriously if you want to fulfill your destiny and see God's Kingdom come! Why?

God doesn't just give you permission to take a break once a week—He also commands you to come into His presence and find rest for your soul. Ceaseless toil wearies even the most ardent soul. God needs his troops in the best possible condition—physically, mentally, emotionally, and spiritually.

If you don't do so already, give yourself a weekly supernatural battery charge by worshiping God and observing the Sabbath.

## DON'T LET MAN'S LAWS KEEP YOU FROM RESTING IN JESUS.

Jesus was a Sabbath keeper who realized the importance of staying in touch with Father God. He knew the burden of religious legalism and challenged Israel's leaders to stop loading down God's people with unnecessary rules and regulations.

The "yoke" (or religious teaching) of Israel's leaders led the people into spiritual poverty, not personal relationships with Father God. Jesus rebuked them for heaping religious burdens on the people and keeping them from entering God's Kingdom. "Woe to you, teachers of the law and Pharisees, you hypocrites! You shut the kingdom of heaven in men's faces. You yourselves do not enter, nor will you let those enter who are trying to" (Matt 23:13).

*That's a serious and substantive accusation.*

The Pharisees, Sadducees, priests, and teachers of the law failed to see, enter, and teach the reality of God's incoming Kingdom. They plotted against God's Son because He didn't fit their preconceived notions of the Messiah. Jesus, however, rallied the common people and felt the weight of the burdens heaped on them by their leaders: temple taxes, inflated prices for sacrificial animals, fees for exchanging common currency for temple currency, and ice-cold legality steeped in centuries of traditions that gradually calcified the once-living faith of first-century Judaism.

Jesus saw weariness in everyone's eyes. He also heard it in their voices—weariness born in the brutality of Roman rule, arduous religious requirements, and centuries of God's silence.

Imagine if you were living in Jerusalem at that time what it would feel like to hear Jesus say to you:

> *Come to Me, all you who are weary and burdened, and I will give you rest. Take My yoke upon you and learn from Me, for I am gentle and humble in heart, and you will find rest for your souls. For My yoke is easy and My burden is light* (Matthew 11:28-30).

You'd feel exhilarated, liberated, and filled with hope!
Your burdens would vanish and rest would flood your soul.
*Jesus is still giving rest to weary Christian warriors.*

If you want to experience His life-enriching rest for your soul, find a quiet place and let Him unload your burdens one by one.

As Charles Spurgeon writes, only Jesus can remove your burdens and bring lasting rest to your soul.

> "The needle that hath been touched with the load-stone may be shaken and agitated, but it never rests until it turns towards the pole." Thus our heart's affections, when once magnetized by the love of Christ,

find no rest except they turn to Him. The cares and labors of the day may carry the thoughts to other objects, even as a finger may turn the needle to the east or west, but no sooner is the pressure removed than the thoughts fly to the well-beloved just as the needle moves to its place. We are unable to rest anywhere but in Jesus.[2]

What is your part in getting rid of your burdens? Apostle Peter makes that perfectly clear when he says to cast onto Jesus "the whole of your care—all your anxieties, all your worries, all your concerns, once and for all—on Him [Jesus]; for He cares for you affectionately, and cares about you watchfully" (1 Peter 5:7 AMP). The New Living Translation says, "Give all your worries and cares to God, for He cares about you."

Isn't this a wonderful promise? Jesus' heart overflows with compassion, and He desires to relieve you of your burdens. He's willing to take all your worries, anxieties, and concerns—every burden you will ever carry—and bear them for you Himself. Just release your burdens to Jesus, and He will calm your restless soul.

## Share One Another's Burdens.

God also asks us to share other people's burdens.

Recently an acquaintance dropped by our home and poured out her heart, disclosing heavy burdens and asking us to walk with her through the dark valley shrouding her weary soul. We consented to pray for her and her family. We couldn't change her circumstances, but we could and did choose to journey with her. Our prayers, friendship, counsel, and love bring her comfort in times of grief. She appreciates us sharing her burdens. We know that Apostle Paul also understands the power of burden sharing because he says to the church in Philippi, "...it was good of you to share in my troubles" (Phil. 4:14).

What motivates us to share burdens? *Agape*, life-transforming, sacrificial love!

It was *agape* that motivated Jesus to take your sins to the cross and *agape* that filled your soul when the Holy Spirit took up residence inside you. You share other people's burdens by loving them just like Jesus loves you. How do you know what this love should be like? Apostle John says:

> *This is how we know what love is: Jesus Christ laid down His life for us. And we ought to lay down our lives for our brothers. If anyone has material possessions and sees his brother in need but has no pity on him, how can the love of God be in him? Dear children, let us not love with words or tongue but with actions and in truth. This then is how we know that we belong to the truth, and how we set our hearts at rest in his presence whenever our hearts condemn us. For God is greater than our hearts, and He knows everything"* (1 John 3:16-20).

In a similar way, Apostle Paul teaches us why it's important to share another's burdens. "Carry each other's burdens, and in this way you will fulfill the law of Christ" (Gal. 6:2).

Love is the "law" of Christ. When you love others enough to help them carry a burden, it lightens their load and brings rest to their souls.

As I was reflecting in my journal on why it's so imperative for us to bear one another's burdens, the Lord shared the following thoughts with me:

> *The burdens of the world result from inner conflict emerging from human hearts. Discontent spurs the worldly appetites of disheartened people. Burdens come from rebelling against my sovereignty. I am a burden bearer. I take upon Myself the pain of the world, its sicknesses, and sadness.*

*Here is why you are disheartened right now. Deep in your heart is a seed of unrest. It was planted in the hearts of men when Adam fell. It is the dark view of life—a bitter root that displaces the wellspring of My love and power in a human heart. Burdens come from discontent, shallow faith, and worldly mindsets.*

*The burdens many bear are less heavy than they realize. The weight of a burden comes from the doubts many have about My goodness. If I'm seen as pure goodness, then My Word is seen as a good Word. It is appreciated by eyes of faith.*

*Mark this—I am good all the time—pure, untainted good. Not marred, no defects, just pure good. So as a Pure Good God, I am dependable, My Word is sure, My promises are kept, and those who follow Me are blessed when they embrace Me and My goodness without doubt.*

*Here is a practical application. Take a young boy whose father is not personable. He demands obedience but provides little concrete guidance or affirmation to his son. The son must guess how to please his father and often falls short of pleasing him because the standard changes. My guidance is specific, and My standard never changes.*

*Burdens develop over time. You focus on a burden that comes from sickness or injury, rebellious children, bills that can't be paid. These too are burdens—but the deepest, most insidious burdens are those that shape the focus of a life. They come into a heart at a young age and weigh down their victims for a lifetime. Abuse, rejection, failure to please a demanding parent, the death of a loved one—all these are significant burdens to carry for a lifetime.*

*I release people from burdens so they may experience the joy and hope I want all my people to know.*

*Take Charge of Your Destiny*
*Principle Twelve:*
*Let God share your burdens.*

## ACTION STEPS

### STEP ONE: RELEASE YOUR BURDENS TO GOD.

Spiritual conflict often brings burdens. It's the enemy's way of distracting your attention from his devious schemes. Our international church's rapid growth has brought the "burdens" of severely limited parking, overcrowded classrooms, multiple services each Sunday, and the need for more staff—not to mention additional funds to rent more space. Along with rapid growth, our congregation has experienced an unusually high number of serious injuries, sicknesses, and surgeries. The devil isn't happy with what God's doing in and through us. How are we dealing with the pressures we're facing?

Prayer, fasting, claiming God's promises, and exuberant worship are our most potent weapons. We fight back! We've discovered that consistently attending to spiritual disciplines often keeps the enemy at bay.

Every Christian faces demonic assaults. That's why we teach our congregations to start and end every day with prayer and Bible study. That's also why we encourage only limited family friendly television viewing and prioritizing home worship and fellowship. But even with that proactive approach, flaming darts still get through.

Recently I awoke during the night with great burdens in my heart and mind. I knew the Lord would release me from them eventually, but as I began praying, I realized my mind and emotions were out of balance with my faith. To find rest for my soul, I spent an hour praying and claiming Scripture. I pictured all my burdens in little boxes on a table and Jesus standing next to me as, one by one, I handed Him the boxes. He lifted the burdens off me. I literally felt weight leave my body and peace fill my soul, and then I fell right to sleep. He's an incredible Savior.

Many harassment burdens will disappear after earnest prayer and worship. Others may take days or weeks to lose their influence in your life. If you carry deep or lifelong burdens that keep weighing you down, you probably need your pastor's help in finding rest for your soul.

## STEP TWO: SHARE OTHER PEOPLE'S BURDENS.

Teamwork is the essential ingredient in most successful initiatives. Kingdom service is no different. Your spiritual and natural gifts determine where you'll make the greatest positive impact for Christ in your home, church, and community.

Do what you can to help those who are struggling. You can lighten someone's burden with a phone call, bouquet of flowers, visit, e-card, hot meal, listening ear, or new friendship. Everyone can do something to help others bear their burdens.

When you hear that someone you know needs help, ask God what He wants you to do, and then do it for His glory. You may not be able to help everyone you know who has a burden, but you can help someone who will benefit from your love and kindness.

## CONCLUSION

In this chapter I've discussed how the enemy tries to weigh you down with burdens and hinder your Kingdom service. Jesus, your burden bearer, is willing and able to help you unload your burdens and enter His rest. He's also calling you to help others bear their burdens.

In the next chapter you'll learn why it's important to cultivate a heart of gratitude for the many blessings God brings into your life. He's calling you to deeper faith and will bring you into the fullness of His anointing as you learn to praise Him in all situations.

### ENDNOTES

1. GIGA Quotes, Sabbath, http://www.giga-usa.com/quotes/topics/sabbath_t001.htm.

2. http://elbourne.org/sermons/index.mv?illustrations+3119.

# CHAPTER 13

# Be Thankful for Everything

*Every good and perfect gift is from above, coming down from the Father of the heavenly lights, who does not change like shifting shadows. He chose to give us birth through the word of truth, that we might be a kind of first-fruits of all He created. —James, the brother of Jesus* (James 1:17-18).

A Christian who walks by faith accepts all circumstances from God. He thanks God when everything goes good, when everything goes bad, and for the "blues" somewhere in-between. He thanks God whether he feels like it or not. —Reverend Erwin W. Lutzer

God is in the blessing business.

That's right! His nature is to bless those who love Him! Like any loving parent, God delights in blessing His faithful family members. It's too bad some people don't see the blessings in their lives as God's gifts. How about you? Are you aware of how God is blessing you?

If not, it's time to realize that every blessing in your life is a gift from God.

## GOD'S GREATEST GIFT

The special quarters unit in a military correctional facility or "brig" is where serious offenders spend 23 hours a day in isolation. As I entered the brig for a pastoral call, I passed the first security checkpoint, surrendered my keys and other items, and was then escorted through two more guarded doorways. Entering the special quarters unit, I was warned by a military police sergeant to stay behind the bright yellow line painted on the cement floor. His demeanor clearly expressed the potential danger of coming within arm's reach of the prisoner I was there to visit.

A young man from my unit was sitting on a mattress cradling his head in his hands. He looked up when I said hello. As I studied his chiseled face, I saw anger in his eyes and clenched jaw. I winced a bit in remembering that his was a violent crime, one almost unimaginable to me.

The sergeant provided a chair, so I sat the requisite distance from the cell door and asked a simple question.

"How can I help you?"

"It's too late for that," he said, studying me.

"You're right. I can't undo what you're in here for, but I can help you with your future."

"What do you mean?" he said after a few moments.

"I know you've been convicted of very serious crimes and will be transferred to prison soon, but since you're still here, let's talk about God's forgiveness."

"Forgiveness?"

"That's right. God's promise of absolute forgiveness."

"Why would he forgive me? I almost killed the guy I beat up, and I hammered an MP. I'll never get out of confinement."

"There are two kinds of prisons—one for your body and one for your heart. I can't do anything about where you'll be spending the foreseeable future, but I can help you get your heart out of prison."

"Really? How?"

Over the next hour I shared the good news of Jesus' life, death, and resurrection with a man whose life was out of control.

He told me about the violence in his childhood home, his dad's drinking problem, his mother abandoning him and his siblings. He was never loved, affirmed, or appreciated by his parents. Instead, they often told him he was a loser. No wonder he was angry.

Enlisting was his way of escaping his toxic family life. He heard sermons in boot camp chapel services but hadn't understood them. Once he finished training and had spare time on his hands, his life fell apart. It was a story I've heard too many times over the years. The night he and some buddies went bar hopping, his life hit bottom. In a drunken rage, he'd almost killed a man who chided him for being a "dumb grunt."

During our conversation, he realized that Jesus was his only hope for a better life. Before I left, he asked God to forgive a lifetime of rebelling against authority, hating his family, and despising himself. Then he gave his heart to Jesus.

*He gratefully received God's gift of eternal life.*

My new brother in Christ faced a stiff sentence, but he's serving it as a Christian with a free heart. God began healing him of the deep soul hurts inflicted on him by his physically abusive father. His future is much brighter than it would have been without Jesus.

Every good and perfect gift is from God (see James 1:17). It's hard to imagine that God's blessing for the young man was going to jail, but I believe he'd tell you imprisonment saved his life. The Lord knew exactly what it would take for a self-loathing, angry abuse victim to surrender his heart to Jesus and receive eternal life.

I was the one who helped him come to Christ, but Jesus was working in his heart long before I arrived. I merely followed the Holy Spirit's leading, and God saved the young man's soul.

*Eternal life in Heaven is God's ultimate gift to humankind.*

Almighty God sent His only Son to save us. When Jesus died on the cross, He conquered death, sin, and the devil. He opened the door to eternal life for all who by faith accept Jesus as their Savior. No one is beyond the grip of God's amazing grace if he or she is willing to humble him or herself and give Jesus his or her heart.

No one is too lost to be saved! That's why Apostle Peter says that "everyone who calls on the name of the Lord will be saved" (Acts 2:21).

If you haven't given Jesus your heart yet, take time to surrender your life to Him right now! His greatest gift is for you to experience eternal life! That won't happen without Jesus' help.

### WHY DO CHRISTIANS EXPERIENCE TRIALS AND TRIBULATION?

Once you've given Jesus your heart, why would God allow you to experience trials and tribulations? Because He loves you unconditionally.

God allows you to face trials and tribulation so you'll become more like Jesus. Not all preachers will tell you this, but it is absolutely true. God disciplines you because He loves you.

He only allows trials to come into your life for your ultimate good. Yes, you can still do something sinful, but you'll reap the negative consequences of your sinful actions. Sin always costs much more than it gives. But when it comes to spiritual development, God has "plans to prosper you and not to harm you, plans to give you hope and a future" (Jer. 29:11). Apostle James tells us:

> *Consider it pure joy, my brothers, whenever you face trials of many kinds, because you know that the testing of your faith develops perseverance. Perseverance must finish its work so that you may be mature and complete, not lacking anything....Blessed is the man who perseveres under trial, because when he has stood the test, he will receive the crown of life that God has promised to those who love Him* (James 1:2-4,12).

Apostle Peter writes with similar sentiment when he says:

*In this you greatly rejoice, though now for a little while you may have had to suffer grief in all kinds of trials. These have come so that your faith—of greater worth than gold, which perishes even though refined by fire—may be proved genuine and may result in praise, glory and honor when Jesus Christ is revealed. Though you have not seen Him, you love Him; and even though you do not see Him now, you believe in Him and are filled with an inexpressible and glorious joy, for you are receiving the goal of your faith, the salvation of your souls* (1 Peter 1:6-9).

It is also God's plan to sometimes allow the devil to test your faith as he did Job's faith. Again Peter has sobering instructions for us:

*Be self-controlled and alert. Your enemy the devil prowls around like a roaring lion looking for someone to devour. Resist him, standing firm in the faith, because you know that your brothers throughout the world are undergoing the same kind of sufferings. And the God of all grace, who called you to His eternal glory in Christ, after you have suffered a little while, will Himself restore you and make you strong, firm and steadfast. To Him be the power for ever and ever. Amen* (1 Peter 5:8-11).

If there was any doubt in your mind that God allows limited trials and tribulation for your good, I hope these passages have convinced you that trials and tribulation are actually gifts from your loving heavenly Father. He knows exactly what your limits are and does not allow anything to come into your life that doesn't first pass through His loving hands.

## What Does Jesus Say About Blessings?

Jesus has a sobering message for all who choose to follow Him. It's sobering because some Christians believe God exists to meet their every want and desire. Jesus promises to meet your needs (see Matt. 6:33), but God's plan is to conform you to the likeness of Jesus. You're called to walk as He walked. Apostle John says, "Whoever claims to live in Him must walk as Jesus did" (1 John 2:6). Jesus lived to give, not to take. Listen to how He defines blessings in Kingdom terms.

- Blessed are the poor in spirit, for theirs is the kingdom of heaven.

- Blessed are those who mourn, for they will be comforted.

- Blessed are the meek, for they will inherit the earth.

- Blessed are those who hunger and thirst for righteousness, for they will be filled.

- Blessed are the merciful, for they will be shown mercy.

- Blessed are the pure in heart, for they will see God.

- Blessed are the peacemakers, for they will be called sons of God.

- Blessed are those who are persecuted because of righteousness, for theirs is the kingdom of heaven.

- Blessed are you when people insult you, persecute you and falsely say all kinds of evil against you because of Me.

- Rejoice and be glad, because great is your reward in heaven, for in the same way they persecuted the prophets who were before you (Matt. 5:3-12).

Jesus is saying that blessings in His terms are different than the world's conception of blessings. The world sees blessings as fame and fortune, power and popularity, while Jesus sees blessings coming to those faithfully serving Him in the midst of persecution, sadness, and deprivation, as well as in less difficult times.

On one hand, Jesus says that the poor in spirit, the meek, those hungering for more of God, the merciful, the pure in heart, and the peacemakers, will be greatly blessed. How? With entry into His Kingdom, with inheriting the Earth, with being filled with God's presence, receiving mercy, seeing God, and being called sons (or daughters) of God.

On the other hand, Jesus says those who mourn are blessed with comfort. Those who are persecuted are blessed with entering the Kingdom of Heaven. Those who are insulted for loving Him are blessed. Those lied about for honoring Him are blessed. Why? Those who are persecuted, insulted, or lied about for loving Jesus will reap unimaginable blessings in Heaven, even if their earthly lives are cut short by martyrdom.

It's apparent from Jesus' teaching that every Christian should be thinking of God's blessings in Kingdom terms, rather than just in earthly terms.

## LIVE IN GRATITUDE FOR GOD'S GIFT OF ETERNAL LIFE.

Once you've professed Jesus as your Savior, then what? Do you just live like the world or does Jesus ask something more of you? He says:

> *As the Father has loved Me, so have I loved you. Now remain in My love. If you obey My commands, you will remain in My love, just as I have obeyed My Father's commands and remain in His love. I have told you this so that My joy may be in you and that your joy may be complete. My command is this: Love each other as I have loved you. Greater love has no one than this, that he lay down his life for his friends. You are My friends if you do what I command"* (John 15:9-14).

Do you want to be Jesus' friend? *Then do what He commands.*

Why? Jesus loves you and desires your love in return. Express your love to Him by doing His will. *Agape* is love in action—it's never passive.

*Agape* is actually an act of your will. It's in your control to love or not to love. Contrary to the picture Hollywood paints, love is not just a romantic feeling; it's a decision, a choice, a sacred response to God's love. It's always within your control to love or not love God, yourself, and others. How does this relate to being thankful for God's blessings?

There's nothing that blesses God more than loving Him and those around you with all your heart! You've received a priceless gift—God's abundant grace. The purest motive for serving God is a spirit of gratitude. Apostle Paul says:

> *God raised us up with Christ and seated us with Him in the heavenly realms in Christ Jesus, in order that in the coming ages He might show the incomparable riches of His grace, expressed in His kindness to us in Christ Jesus. For it is by grace you have been saved, through faith—and this not from yourselves, it is the gift of God* (Ephesians 2:6-8).

*Praise God for His gift of grace!*

Few people have cherished God's free gift of grace more than former slave ship captain John Newton. In his early years he was kidnapped and drafted into the British Navy. Undaunted by the seeming impossibility of escaping from indentured service, he attempted to escape but was soon apprehended and stripped of his midshipman rank. As a lowly deckhand, John was treated brutally until he was finally allowed to transfer to a slave ship. There he excelled in abusing his human cargo.

One night, as a violent storm pounded his fragile vessel, he prayed for God's mercy. His ship miraculously stayed afloat, and his heart began its voyage toward Jesus. So thankful was John for the blessing of salvation and the gift of God's unmerited grace that he penned one of Christendom's most unforgettable hymns, "Amazing Grace, how sweet the sound that saved a wretch like me. I once was lost, but now am found, was blind, but now, I see..."

*Cultivate a deep appreciation for your salvation.*

It's easy to see your hope of eternal life as "fire" insurance—but it's so much more than that. Your salvation is a treasure of incalculable worth. It was purchased by the blood of God's only son.

## BE THANKFUL FOR GOD'S BLESSINGS.

A beautiful sunrise, cardinals chirping, waves crashing along a rocky coastline, your favorite pet's playful antics, greeting cards filled with warm sentiments, and visits with special friends. God brings blessings into your life with enough frequency to uplift you, but He won't spoil you into taking Him for granted. Tough times and less stressful times both bring blessings. One, the blessing of stronger faith, the other, moments of unexpected joy lifting your spirit and bringing you hope and gladness.

I'm moved by Apostle Paul's admonition to the Christians in Philippi when he says:

> *Do not be anxious about anything, **but in everything, by prayer and petition, with thanksgiving, present your requests to God**. And the peace of God, which transcends all understanding, will guard your hearts and your minds in Christ Jesus* (Philippians 4:6-7).

As one given to occasional negative thoughts, I find it a great blessing to retune my mind with praise. It's putting into practice the "with thanksgiving" part of Paul's teaching, which buoys my spirit when the pressures of ministry weigh on my mind. I find God releases me from the torment of "what ifs" as long as I thank Him for all things—including the trials and tribulation that come unexpectedly and inconveniently into my life.

God knows that your life is difficult at times. He wants you to let go of the things He's willing to handle for you. Thank Him in the glad times and in sad times. Praise Him when things are going well and when you're facing trials and tribulations. Let the Holy Spirit rule in your heart and heal you of anything distracting you from seeing God's blessings unfold around you.

The Lord gave me these reflections early one morning as I was dealing with my tendency to fret over things outside my control:

*Don't fret over what you don't have; rejoice in what you do have. I am your provider, and I will bring to you all you need. Don't fret about what others have; remember that you know very little about their lives. Many people carry burdens you don't have to carry because you follow Me, so rejoice in what you already have and be content with that. You may think that this life consists in the abundance of material things; it doesn't. The greatest things you can hope for in this life are salvation, peace of mind, joy, love, and lasting friendships. Let Me bring blessings to you as I deem you ready to receive them. Keep your eyes fixed on things above and you'll have much more joy as a result.*

*Take Charge of Your Destiny
Principle Thirteen:
Every blessing in your life is a gift from God.*

## ACTION STEPS

### STEP ONE: THANK GOD WHEN THINGS GO WELL.

Too many people take God's blessings for granted. Freedom of worship, the right to own a Bible, prayer, and fellowship with other believers are easily overlooked as God's blessings by those not being persecuted for their faith. Hundreds of other blessings are yours every day, yet you may miss them if you're preoccupied with worries, discontentment, dissatisfaction, and unfulfilled earthly longings. Don't let the world steal your awareness of God's blessings.

Take time every day to thank God for life's large and small blessings. How? Take satisfaction in what you have already, and resist the temptation to covet more than you need. Sing praises to God—He knows the desires of your heart as well as the down side of fulfilling all of your desires. God will give you enough for a good and satisfying life, but not so much that unwanted complications tag along as a result.

> *Follow apostle Paul's advice and you'll experience much more joy and satisfaction in your life.* **"Be joyful always; pray continually; give thanks in all circumstances, for this is God's will for you in Christ Jesus"** *(1 Thessalonians 5:16-18).*

### STEP TWO: THANK GOD FOR TRIALS AND TRIBULATION.

When I was a seminarian, I read Chaplain Merlin Carothers' book, *Prison to Praise,* in which he encourages his readers to thank God for everything, including trials and tribulation. I was so moved by the testimonies in his book that I decided to praise God in all situations. What I discovered was amazing. First, I found that God often intercedes in difficult situations when I acknowledge His sovereignty by praising and thanking Him. Second, I found that I had more faith to deal with difficult situations and often received spiritual insights that brought me quickly through the darkness back into the light.

Paul says, "Give thanks in all circumstances, for this is God's will for you in Christ Jesus" (1 Thess. 5:18). He means *all* circumstances. When he saw masses of conversions, he gave thanks *and* when he was imprisoned for preaching the Gospel, he also gave thanks. Praise freed him from tormenting spirits.

It may seem counterintuitive to thank God when tragedy strikes. God isn't the author of premature death, prolonged illness, or shocking events. They are a product of the fallen nature of man and natural events. When your life falls apart, it's essential that you don't blame God, but turn to Him for solace and strength. He alone is your strength and your salvation. As King David tells us, "God is our refuge and strength, always ready to help in times of trouble" (Ps. 46:1 NLT). When we thank God in all situations, it is a declaration of faith in God's sovereignty and unwavering love.

Many things happen that have no explanation on this side of eternity. One thing is sure—Jesus promises to be with us in the presence of his comforting Holy Spirit until the end of time (see Matt. 28:20).

Do your best to give thanks for the "good" things and for the "not so good" things that come into your life. Give thanks for your cranky co-worker, your rebellious teen, and your loneliness. Why? In doing so you are releasing God's supernatural power and presence into the situation. You're giving it to Him to take for action. You're acknowledging that your heavenly Father is sovereign Lord of the universe.

Meditate on the following passage for a week. I hope and pray it will help you cultivate a sense of wonder as God opens your spiritual eyes to the many blessings He has in store for you. Paul writes to the church in Rome:

*And we know that **in all things God works for the good of those who love Him, who have been called according to His purpose.** For those God foreknew He also predestined to be conformed to the likeness of His Son, that He might be the firstborn among many brothers. ...For I am convinced that neither death nor life, neither angels nor demons, neither the present nor the future, nor any powers, neither height nor depth, nor anything else in all creation, will be able to separate us from the love of God that is in Christ Jesus our Lord* (Romans 8:28-29;38-39).

## CONCLUSION

In this chapter I've challenged you to thank God for the many blessings He brings into your life. The world's idea of blessings rarely includes trials and tribulations that make a Christian's faith stronger. You can't make that mistake. Every good and perfect gift comes from God. In thanking Him for all things, you acknowledge His sovereignty and release His presence and power into seemingly unsolvable situations.

In the final chapter I'll focus on how you can change the world by looking for opportunities to pray for those around you. When you pray for others, God's power flows through you into those for whom you are praying. As God moves through you, His Kingdom power and glory flow from Heaven into the hearts of those in your circle of influence and beyond.

# CHAPTER 14

# Pray for Others

*And this is my prayer: that your love may abound more and more in knowledge and depth of insight, so that you may be able to discern what is best and may be pure and blameless until the day of Christ, filled with the fruit of righteousness that comes through Jesus Christ—to the glory and praise of God. —Apostle Paul Praying for the Church in Philippi* (Philippians 1:9-11)

God shapes the world by prayer. The more praying there is in the world, the better the world will be, the mightier the forces against evil.... The prayers of God's saints are the capital stock of Heaven by which God carries on His great work upon earth. God conditions the very life and prosperity of His cause on prayer. —E.M. Bounds

Prayer is the lifeblood of dynamic Christian faith. It's ongoing communication with God through which He transforms the world. The power of prayer unleashes revivals and societal transformation. It heals ailing bodies, refocuses distracted minds, and energizes sluggish spirits. Do you know people who need God? Keep praying for Him to move in their lives.

Pray often, expect results, and don't quit! Why?

*Your prayers change the world one life at a time.*

## MAKE PRAYER A DAILY DISCIPLINE.

At 6 A.M. on Tuesday mornings, my wife and I gather with a small group to pray for the needs of our congregation and community. We begin with singing and Bible reading and then intercede for those God has placed in our sphere of influence— fellow leaders; the infirmed, struggling, and unsaved; church members; those in harm's way; and many others. We move more deeply into God's presence as we pray. He fills our hearts with love and brings us into His sacred sanctuary. At times He releases a word of prophecy or encouragement. Time flies by.

On the days we don't have early morning prayer at church, Sally and I invest 30 to 45 minutes in morning devotions and prayer before tackling our day's work. We listen to God more than we petition Him. As He directs our thoughts to Scripture passages and specific needs, we intercede for others He brings to mind as well as those we pray for daily.

In Chapter 1, I discussed the need for you to listen attentively to God if you want to discover the ultimate meaning of your life. Why? Because God imparts His instructions and wisdom to those whose hearts are attentive to Him. The key to hearing God speak is taking the time to listen for Him. He will always communicate in ways you will understand.

Along with receiving specific instructions and wisdom from God, you also need to covenant with God in looking for opportunities to pray for those around you. This chapter will focus on the practical aspects of interceding for those in your circle of influence.

## ASK GOD FOR OPPORTUNITIES TO PRAY FOR OTHERS.

How did Jesus know what Father God wanted Him to do? He rose early for prayer and fellowship with His Father. That's when Father God encouraged, instructed, and empowered Jesus for ministry, one day at a time.

Jesus restricted Himself to doing God's will in the same ways He expects you to do it. That's in the power of the Holy Spirit as God brings you opportunities to minister in His name, for His glory. Jesus' ministry wasn't program focused, routine, or contrived. He simply joined what He saw Father God doing at the time. Jesus says:

*I tell you the truth, the Son can do nothing by Himself; He can do only what He sees his Father doing, because **whatever the Father does the Son also does. For the Father loves the Son and shows Him all He does.** Yes, to your amazement He will show Him even greater things than these* (John 5:19-20).

If the Son of God worked in concert with Father God and didn't initiate ministry without the Father's leading, you should do no less if you hope to bring God's Kingdom to Earth by doing His will. God is always at work around you, but He won't always invite you to join Him in what He's doing. If you're available to Him, He'll certainly invite you to partner in His work when it suits His purposes for your life. It's up to God to open your eyes, ears, and heart to what He's up to and equip you to fulfill your role in His plans.

God always makes His will clear if He knows you're going to do it!

*Are you ready to do what God has planned for you?*

Recently I was at our church to lead a new members' class, but only one of our new members was able to attend that evening. I wasn't sure what to do until the only person to show up asked me a question about marital relationships. I sensed God at work and realized we weren't there to discuss church membership. For over an hour we shared the Word and discussed issues that emerged as a result. It was a divinely inspired meeting.

Have you had occasions like that? You know—when you planned something and God moved in a completely different direction? Were you flexible enough to deal with it even if you spent hours preparing a presentation or you had a tight schedule and had to reschedule an appointment? Did you reprioritize your time and let the Spirit move through you in His perfect way?

You take charge of your destiny when you align your life with the will of God. That may mean your plans have to change! Why? Father God's plans must take priority even if they're inconvenient for you!

When Jesus met the woman at the well and spoke about her sordid history, He and His companions were on their way home to Galilee. They took the shortcut through Samaria rather than traveling through the Decapolis. It was probably their plan to move quickly through Gentile territory, since they'd been away from home for an extended time. Father God had a different plan. Jesus was so focused on doing God's will as it was unfolding before Him that He didn't even want to eat lunch.

> *"My food," said Jesus, "is to do the will of Him who sent Me and to finish his work. Do you not say, 'Four months more and then the harvest'? I tell you, open your eyes and look at the fields! They are ripe for harvest. Even now the reaper draws his wages, even now he harvests the crop for eternal life, so that the sower and the reaper may be glad together. Thus the saying 'One sows and another reaps' is true. I sent you to reap what you have not worked for. Others have done the hard work, and you have reaped the benefits of their labor." Many of the Samaritans from that town believed in him because of the woman's testimony, "He told me everything I ever did." So when the Samaritans came to Him, they urged Him to stay with them,*

*and He stayed two days. And because of His words many more became believers* (John 4:34-41).

*The salvation of many souls might have been lost if Jesus hadn't been attuned to His Father's will.*

Paul and his traveling companions had an experience of planning to do one thing and being led by the Holy Spirit to do another. Luke writes:

*Paul and his companions traveled throughout the region of Phrygia and Galatia, having been kept by the Holy Spirit from preaching the word in the province of Asia. When they came to the border of Mysia, they tried to enter Bithynia, but the Spirit of Jesus would not allow them to. So they passed by Mysia and went down to Troas. During the night Paul had a vision of a man of Macedonia standing and begging him, "Come over to Macedonia and help us"' After Paul had seen the vision, we got ready at once to leave for Macedonia, concluding that God had called us to preach the gospel to them"* (Acts 16:6-10).

*God interrupted Paul's life to ensure he stayed in the center of His will.*

If you're willing to do what God asks of you, He will make His will so clear you won't be able to miss it. So here's a practical application.

Pray every morning, "Lord I'm willing to do anything you want me to do, anywhere, anytime, for anyone. Amen."

Then stay attuned to the Spirit as you go about your day expecting God to show you what He's doing and watching for opportunities to join Him in His work.

## HOW TO RECOGNIZE WHAT GOD IS DOING AROUND YOU

God will set up situations for you to touch others with His love. So keep your eyes and ears open for opportunities to pray for those around you. You won't always be sure if God has set up a situation in advance. That's why you should ask Him to make His movements clear to you.

Recently, I had the opportunity to pray with some Senate staffers. God arranged our lives to intersect for a few precious moments, and they were glad for me to pray with and for them. I have these occasions daily on Capitol Hill, but with strangers, it's a different story.

Recently, as I was walking to my METRO stop, I found myself keeping stride with a congresswoman. I said hello to her. I was checking to see if God had set up a situation where I could engage her in meaningful conversation. As we walked along, she pulled out her blackberry and started reading e-mails. I realized immediately that she was not interested in chatting with me, so I picked up my pace and prayed for her as I continued on my way.

After boarding my train, a young married woman sat down beside me. I tested the waters with her by asking how her day was going. She said, "Fine," and then pulled out a book and started reading. I was sitting there praying for God to give me an opening, but it didn't happen. I prayed for her for a few more minutes and then starting jotting notes for this chapter.

*Don't worry about failing God if someone doesn't want to discuss faith issues with you. He values your willingness to serve even when nothing substantive happens.*

As I exited my train and walked upstairs toward the parking garage, I noticed a recovering stroke victim slowly but surely ascending the stairs ahead of me. I reached the top of the staircase at the same time he did. I felt compassion surge through me so I gently patted his back and said, "You're doing great!" He smiled and said, "Thanks a lot," obviously thrilled to have regained the ability to use his affected leg and climb stairs. It was a quick encounter, but I sensed the Holy Spirit move through me when I touched his back. It's up to God to continue the process of loving the man into the Kingdom if he's not a Christian already.

Look for opportunities to pray for others—directly or silently. Your prayers will positively impact the lives of those around you. But what if it seems like your prayers have little or no effect?

*Keep praying even if you're tempted to believe your prayers have no positive effect.*

God is the only one who can save a soul, heal a sick or broken body, or deliver an oppressed person from demonic influence. He can do it sovereignly or through yielded human hearts. It's His choice.

Your job is to live in love and stay alert for the Holy Spirit's subtle promptings. Expect God to interrupt your life when He has a Kingdom assignment for you.

### KEEP PACE WITH GOD.

It's very important to keep pace with God and not force yourself on others in a desperate attempt to win them to Christ, pray for them, or get them into your church. Let the Lord set up opportunities for you to share His love with others as He moves ahead of you.

I teach our church members not to waste time witnessing to those who show absolutely no interest in God, but to pray for divine appointments with those the Lord is wooing to Himself.

It doesn't take long to discover whether people want to discuss spiritual things. When they do, it's a much wiser investment of your limited time to engage those whose hearts are being warmed by the Holy Spirit. Once you see that they're open to God, keep praying for them to "see and understand" who Jesus is and what He's done on their behalf.

A few decades ago, I returned to my first seminary to attend a series of lectures. A visiting professor gave us the following advice about witnessing for Christ:

Suppose you were a mole, comfortable with darkness and secure in your tiny den. Would you be inclined to leave your familiar surroundings if someone shined a 10,000 watt spotlight in your face? Of course not! But if you peeked out of your hole into the darkness and saw a single candle light you may be curious enough to investigate it because it doesn't appear threatening. Give others your love and let God touch others with your life as well as your words. Only give others what God has for them. If you beat them up with your words, they'll close their hearts to you. If you love them unconditionally, they'll see Jesus in your life and be attracted to Him through your love. Then they'll be open to what you have to say.[1]

I think this advice is still relevant. Some people will engage you in conversation in a vain attempt to prove that their intellectually superior ideas transcend the truth of Scripture. Others enjoy sin and feel threatened by those who don't live as they do, so once they find out you're a Christian, they'll walk away. Then there are those who've been fed a steady diet of anti-God rhetoric for so long that they've stopped thinking for themselves. Though many of these people may seem to be listening to you when you attempt to witness to them, they're actually blind and deaf to the things of God.

Prayer can break the spiritual forces holding them captive, but it's generally futile to quibble over ideas about God with those who don't believe in God.

The Lord usually gives me two or three substantive witnessing opportunities a week. Just a few days ago, I was pleasantly surprised to have three brief spiritual conversations in just ten minutes. Each of the individuals accepted my invitation to attend our weekly Senate staff Bible study. They may not see their attending a Bible study as I do—a step toward God—but that's exactly what it is. They've accepted the challenge to study

God's Word and in doing so have placed themselves in a position of seeking Him. God rewards earnest seekers (see Heb. 11:6).

### Ask Others If You May Pray for Them.

My wife has grown bold in her encounters with people in need. She'll listen with compassion and then ask whether she may pray for them. Almost no one refuses. Sometimes it's a plumber, store clerk, neighbor, or a friend. She loves bringing their concerns to the throne of grace and helping them realize that Jesus loves them and cares for them in their suffering. She's committed to looking for opportunities to pray for those around her.

On many Saturday afternoons, our church members visit the neighborhoods within a mile or two of our facility. They have no agenda or quotas. What they do have is love to share in whatever ways God brings to them. Scores of opportunities to pray for others come from walking around neighborhoods, visiting stores, and just being available to God.

During our church's recent neighborhood clothing giveaway, our Spanish pastor and his dedicated outreach team offered prayer, food, water, and love to our neighbors. Our teams aren't as concerned about people joining our church as they are about seeing our neighbors give their hearts to Jesus. If seekers are interested in our church, we welcome them with open arms. If not, we'll refer them to a congregation that will meet their needs. All of our church's outreach programs are Spirit-led and undergirded by dozens of prayer warriors who gather every weekday morning at 5:30 A.M. and on Saturdays at 7 A.M. for intercessory prayer.

As I was journaling in preparation for writing this concluding chapter, the Lord said to me:

> *My life-giving power is released through the prayers of My faithful followers. Too often, the world steals your time and distracts you from My purposes. Fight for sacred intimacy,*

*and give Me your heart. Let Me direct your intercession and move in the power of My Spirit.*

*Prayer is the critical element in Kingdom warfare. Prayer has power to destroy strongholds and bring My Kingdom to Earth. Don't be distracted by a busy world; give Me your heart and allow Me to use your prayers to establish My Kingdom on Earth. I will dethrone sickness and oppression through your prayers. I will bring revival through your prayers. I will bring order out of chaos and life out of death through your prayers.*

*Pray! Pray often and pray with Heaven in mind. Pray as if your prayers will change the world—they will—one heart at a time. Pray often, pray earnestly for those around you, and pray for My Kingdom to come where My will is done. Pray!*

*Take Charge of Your Destiny*
*Principle Fourteen:*
*Look for opportunities to pray*
*for those around you.*

## ACTION STEPS

### STEP ONE: TRUST GOD TO BLESS YOUR SERVICE.

Don't be surprised when God is moving in someone else's life. Sometimes people you consider the most unlikely to give their hearts to Jesus are the ones closest to doing so. Imagine what the early Christians were thinking about Saul (whose other name is Paul) as he was violently persecuting the Church. Very few people, if any, believed he'd ever become a Christian. Imagine their surprise when he started preaching the Kingdom message just a few days after his conversion (see Acts 9).

You're one of God's front-line warriors in the battle for souls. He'll equip you for everything He's calling you to do, so trust Him to bring you success in Kingdom service. God's plan is for His Kingdom to come where you do His will. Expect Him to reveal His will and empower you to do it for His glory. Then you'll see Him move in the lives of those around you in life altering ways.

### STEP TWO: PRAY FOR OTHERS.

"Pray continually," Paul says (see 1 Thess. 5:17). A lifestyle of prayer leads to living beyond your expectations. God has bigger plans for your life than you do!

During a recent trip to New England, the Lord was definitely at work preparing opportunities for my wife and me to pray for wait staff, hotel clerks, family members, and others. We were amazed at how often those around us gladly accepted our offer to pray for their needs.

Take time to pray for those around you because God will touch them where He sees their greatest needs.

## CONCLUSION

Prayer clarifies the best courses of action in the midst of multiple possibilities. You'll experience the Holy Spirit doing many miracles and see other exciting moves of God when you take time to pray for others. Let prayer guide you to those in need, and then pray for God to meet the needs He makes apparent. The world will become a better place when you pray for those around you.

I pray that you've been challenged to take charge of your destiny. God is calling you to bring His Kingdom to Earth one heart at a time. Your willingness to live for God's glory and do what He's asking of you will make a profound impact on others. In the next few pages you'll find a brief conclusion as well as a summary of the action steps outlined in each chapter of this book.

May the Lord bless you and keep you in the center of His grace as you seek Him daily and live in the center of His will for your life.

### ENDNOTE

1. Dr. Helmut Thielke, Swartly Lecture series, Eastern Baptist Theological Seminary, Philadelphia, circa 1983.

# *Postscript*

This book was conceived in God's mind years before it was given to me. On January 20, 2005, my wife and I, joined three other couples for dinner. Our fellow diners are Christians whose names, positive reputations, and spiritual gifts are well known in the Christian world. During dinner, God moved four of them to prophesy over my wife, Sally, and me for more than an hour. It was the first time in our lives we've received such a detailed, multi-faceted message from God. The transcript of the prophetic utterances totals 12 single-spaced pages.

This book was prophesied that evening. In part, Prophet Hank Kunneman from Lord of Hosts Church in Omaha, Nebraska, said:

> The Lord says that you need to keep up; that you need to keep a journal by your bed because the Lord says, "I'm going to visit you…I'm going to visit you in dreams." The Spirit of the Lord says that when you open your eyes the first thing in the morning…God says to watch now for a period of nine months that I visit thee by way of dreams. God says that even visions in the night hour; but the Lord says that when you open your eyes you will hear an utterance, you will hear a sentence, you will hear a decree. The Lord says write it down because these are things that must go into that which you must write…

208 TAKE CHARGE OF YOUR DESTINY

From January to September 2005, I received 14 spiritual dreams with specific decrees that I recorded in my journal. The decrees God gave me are the thesis statements for each chapter and the **Take Charge of Your Destiny Principles** found at the end of each chapter. From September 2005 to November 2006 I prayed about writing *Take Charge of Your Destiny*. In mid-November 2006, the Lord gave me the green light to begin. The chapters have been written in the order I received the dream statements. The decrees God gave me are also worded exactly as I recorded them. During the course of my labors, the Lord provided prophetic insights into each decree, which I also recorded in my daily journaling. He directed me to focus on specific insights and obstacles related to bringing His Kingdom to earth. I pray these reflections help you discover and live in your destiny so you will see God's Kingdom come where you do His will, for His glory.

Thank you for taking the time to read *Take Charge of Your Destiny*. May you experience an ever-increasing sense of God's presence, anointing, and affirmation in the days ahead.

May His Kingdom come where you do His will on earth as it is done in Heaven. Come Lord Jesus.

Dr. Alan N. Keiran
Springfield, Virginia
July 2008

# Take Charge of Your Destiny
# Action Steps Summary

See chart on following pages.

TAKE CHARGE OF YOUR DESTINY ACTION STEPS SUMMARY

| | Chapter Title | Take Charge of Your Destiny Principles | Take Charge of Your Destiny Action Steps |
|---|---|---|---|
| 1 | Listen to God | Unless you listen attentively to God, your life will have no ultimate meaning. | Make time to listen to God. Expect God to surprise you. |
| 2 | Don't Be Deceived | Fix your eyes on Jesus and you will avoid moral failure. | Resist temptation. Avoid the near occasion of sin. |
| 3 | Live God's Way | You can't have your way and God's way at the same time. | Pray daily for wisdom and power. Read and study God's Word daily. Commit to living God's way. |
| 4 | Use Your Authority | The devil doesn't have any power over you that you can't overcome with the authority of Christ. | Use your spiritual authority. Give God credit for every victory. |
| 5 | Don't Be Hasty | Don't be hasty and you'll avoid many of the pitfalls that negatively affect other people's lives. | Think and pray before you speak and act. Live at a savoring pace. Wait for God's best. |
| 6 | Care for Others | Care for those around you. | Listen and speak graciously. Serve others joyfully. Practice extravagant giving. |
| 7 | Partner With God | You never run the race alone; God is with you all the way. | Partner with God in prayer. Partner with God in worship. Partner with God in Kingdom service. |

## TAKE CHARGE OF YOUR DESTINY ACTION STEPS SUMMARY

| | Chapter Title | Take Charge of Your Destiny Principles | Take Charge of Your Destiny Action Steps |
|---|---|---|---|
| 8 | Expect God's Provision | God will provide what you need to do His will. | Seek God's will. Obey God immediately. Expect God's provision. |
| 9 | Cherish God's Gift of Joy | Don't be so concerned about the future that you miss the joys of the moment. | Confess your worries as sin. Live in day-tight compartments. |
| 10 | Keep Seeking God | Seek God and you will find Him; He's waiting for you. | Seek God every day. Guard your destiny. Practice self-control. |
| 11 | Embrace Humility | Don't try to do everything by yourself; let others help you. | Humbly ask for forgiveness. Humbly offer forgiveness. Ask others to help you. |
| 12 | Release Your Burdens | Let God share your burdens. | Release your burdens to God. Share other people's burdens. |
| 13 | Be Thankful for Everything | Every blessing in your life is a gift from God. | Thank God when things go well. Thank God for trials and tribulations. |
| 14 | Pray for Others | Look for opportunities to pray for those around you. | Trust God to bless your service. Pray for others. |

# Taking Charge of My Life

# Author and Ministry Information

Dr. Alan N. Keiran
Dunamis International Ministries
7103 Danford Place
Springfield, VA 22152

To schedule Alan for a speaking engagement or for information about upcoming *Take Charge of Your Destiny* conferences:

E-mail Alan at: alan_keiran@yahoo.com,
or visit: www.dunamis7.com.